Great Naval Actions

By same author, published by David & Charles
NELSON'S BATTLES

Great Naval Actions

of the
British Navy 1588-1807 and 1916

OLIVER WARNER

Crane, Russak & Company Inc New York

Acknowledgements for kind permission to reproduce the photographs are made in the captions and the following abbreviations are used:
NMMG: *National Maritime Museum, Greenwich*
NPG: *National Portrait Gallery, London*
IWM: *Imperial War Museum, London.*

The diagram showing the Siege of Manila comprises information published by Dr Nicholas Tracy in *The Mariner's Mirror,* with his kind permission. The drawing of the gun turret and handing room is adapted from *From the Dreadnought to Scapa Flow* by Arthur Marder.

© Oliver Warner 1976
First published 1976 by David & Charles
(Publishers) Limited
Brunel House, Newton Abbot, Devon

Published in the United States of America by
Crane, Russak & Company, Inc
347 Madison Avenue
New York, New York 10017
(ISBN 0–8448–1015–0)
Library of Congress Catalog Number 76–28568

Set in 12 on 13 point Bembo and printed in Great Britain at the Alden Press, Oxford

Contents

Introduction

Except for Jutland, the single instance which falls within the age of steam, the actions which find a place in the chapters which follow are linked either in general theme – such as the rise of Dutch and the decline of Spanish sea power or the importance of the Baltic – or in respect of careers and personalities. Although famous actions are included (such as the Armada, Anson's capture of the treasure galleon, and the Glorious First of June), it is hoped that new emphasis may have added something to the background of these events. Lesser-known subjects include the capture of Manila by the British towards the end of the Seven Years' War. The actions which took place off Cape St Vincent and the separate assaults on Copenhagen during the early years of the nineteenth century have been included because confusion has sometimes arisen about episodes differing both in time and circumstances.

As for Jutland, seldom can a single incident have had such a profound effect on the course of a battle (in which thousands of men and and the fleets of two great nations were involved) as that in which Major Harvey of the Royal Marines was concerned. Consideration of a scene on board the *Lion* at the start of the action affords much insight into what followed.

Naval actions entail crises in which differences are sometimes as remarkable as similarities. It is hoped that the contrasts included herein, covering as they do events from the sixteenth century to within living memory, will suggest something of the scope and variety of sea warfare.

As the present work has not involved original research, a great debt is involved to that of others. This is acknowledged in a preface to the bibliography.

O.W.

1 The Spanish Armada and Dutch Help

After the dispersal of the Spanish armada in 1588 the Dutch, who rivalled the English in the measure of their rejoicing and even struck medals of jubilation at the event, may well have felt that their own part in the sea campaign had not been given sufficient credit. Undoubtedly it has been minimised in many appraisals. Yet it was the existence of Dutch sea power which made it certain that until and unless the Spaniards gained an overwhelming victory over the English fleet the Duke of Parma's army in the Netherlands, which had been designed by Philip II to cross the Channel and invade England, had no chance whatever of so doing.

Had Parma been ready it is likely that such an invasion would have been attempted, although Philip's principal object, which he stated in a letter which was returned to him unopened, was not so much outright conquest as the restoration of Catholicism in England, or, at the very least, its full toleration. He sought cessation of English aid to Netherlanders in revolt against his rule and recompense for injuries already done him. These instructions were to remain in the cabin of the Duke of Medina Sidonia's flagship, the *San Martin*, until they could be handed to Parma. The two leaders were not then to meet, thanks to the united efforts of the English and the much smaller Dutch fleet, so the seal stayed unbroken.

The foundation of a regular Dutch navy, one day to rank among the most formidable in the world, belongs essentially to William the Silent, Count of Nassau and Prince of Orange. It was he who, as early as 1569, legitimatised the hitherto piratical *gueux des mers* (the active and much-feared 'Sea Beggars' of the northern provinces of the Netherlands) by allowing them to fly his flag as privateers.

This act did not appreciably alter the lawless tinge of much of Dutch behaviour at sea. Even ten years later, Queen Elizabeth was outraged to hear that Dutchmen had boarded an English ship only six miles from Dover, robbing and stripping the young Earl of Oxford to his shirt. Yet, by virtue of his title as sovereign prince

Queen Elizabeth I (1533–1603)
miniature by Nicholas Hilliard NPG

of a region in the far south of France, remote from the scene of Dutch activity, William was exercising a right which was to become of great and increasing importance. He issued commissions to the principal captains of the Beggars, authorising them to display the lion of Nassau on a flag of three longitudinal stripes – orange, white and blue. The emblem – markedly contrasting with the skull and crossbones associated with piracy – was soon to become known and feared far beyond northern waters. The Beggars even complicated the maritime history of France after Admiral Coligny, the Huguenot leader, had encouraged them to use the port of La Rochelle as a base. This they did under the guidance of William's brother, Louis. Admiral Coligny himself died in 1572 in the massacre of St Bartholomew, the Parisian blood-bath of Protestants which shocked Europe, but not before the facilities he offered had added appreciably to the experience of the Dutch seamen.

Very soon after the time of the armada, the Dutch were to develop and, indeed, almost to mass-produce ship types to sail the multifarious routes they frequented. In earlier days they depended

William the Silent, Prince of Orange
(1533–84)   *Adrien Key*
Rijksmuseum, Amsterdam

much, particularly for inshore work, on two-masted vessels, about sixty feet in length. These were able to mount fair-sized guns; and the Beggars also favoured a smaller build of coaster, single-masted, which again could be adapted for the purpose of war. Dutch skill and ingenuity in the use of sea, estuary, river and canal was limitless. When they could employ their talents against enemies and oppressors, they did so with additional zest. Accounts of their activities often make use of the loose, though descriptive, term 'fly-boats' to cover their handier vessels. In later times it was applied to a regular pattern of small three-master, versions of which may have been employed in earlier decades.

The year that Coligny met his death in Paris, the Beggars, by chance, gained a base at Brill, on one of the outer islands of the estuary of the Meuse. Queen Elizabeth, who was then under pressure from Spain, had forbidden the rebels the use of her ports, and a flotilla of five and twenty sail, under Guillaume de la Marck and battered by spring gales, were forced to find shelter in a part of their own coast, which was in Spanish hands.

The Spanish garrison at Brill had been temporarily called away for duty elsewhere, and as the inhabitants welcomed the Beggars, the booty they brought in to the port, and the 700 or 800 fighting men whom de la Marck commanded, the seamen took possession of town as well as harbour and planted the orange tricolour on the walls. It was the first time that William's flag had flown on dry land in the Netherlands, and there it stayed.

The prince himself was not at first pleased at the incident. He was away at Dillenburg, seeking help from German Protestant princes. William believed he could not afford a haphazard gain such as was apt to bring about damaging reprisals, and de la Marck had been in many scrapes before. Louis, who had been at La Rochelle with most of the rest of the Beggars' fleet, had no such inhibitions. When the news from Brill reached him, he seized Flushing, which raised the tricolour on 6 April 1572.

The approaches to Antwerp, by far the greatest centre of trade in northern Europe, were now threatened. Rotterdam, Schiedam and Gouda followed the lead. Even Alva, Parma's ruthless predecessor, began to realise what he was up against when the herald he sent to Flushing was received neither with violence nor submission, but with ribald laughter. 'Let the Duke come himself,' were the words with which the messenger was greeted. 'We'll eat him alive!'

Such assurance was premature, yet Alva had received a serious blow. Antwerp itself was then far too strong to be in danger, but its flow of merchandise began to diminish. Before the advent of the Beggars to Flushing, there had been at least a thousand resident merchants, Spaniards, Danes, Hanse, Italians, English, Portuguese and Germans among them, dealing with the arrival and the cargoes of 500 ships a day, and with the first bourse in Europe in which to conduct their business. If that flood of life-giving commerce was checked, distress would follow.

Apart from the lodgement of the Beggars to seaward of the port, the city had suffered grievously from riots and from more long-term alarms. The inhabitants had seen the desecration of the cathedral, rich in Catholic trophies, in a Protestant 'Fury' which had raged beyond containment. Afterwards they suffered Spanish and even French 'Furies' when the Duke of Anjou, fishing in troubled waters to try to carve out an independent kingdom for himself, allied himself with William. This complicated matters in the more turbulent areas of the Netherlands, making Anjou detested in the process.

Guillaume de la Marck soon showed that success had not altered his ways. He remained insubordinate, even murderous, and he never acted with any motive other than plunder; he was not a man who could be valued by any responsible authority, least of all by William. He was imprisoned for misconduct, and the task of trying to instil some discipline and to foster some sort of organisation within the Beggars' fleet fell upon other captains, such as Dirk Sonnoy, who was one day to relieve Leyden by a notable feat of arms, and Louis Boisot. Louis of Nassau was fully occupied in land campaigning, otherwise he would have been the natural choice.

Little more than a year after the occupation of Brill and Flushing, the Beggars had another significant success. They out-manœuvred a Spanish fleet off Enkhuysen, on the waters of the Zuider Zee, where they themselves were so much at home and the enemy at such a disadvantage. The Spaniards were all either scattered, sunk or captured, the Beggars towing three large ships and four smaller ones to the security of their own havens.

Among the prizes was a flagship mounting thirty-two fine bronze cannon. The person of the admiral was also secured. He was the Count of Bossu, an important dignitary who made a useful hostage. His capture helped to ensure better treatment for prisoners of war, who had hitherto been dealt with mercilessly.

News of the reverse at sea had hardly been digested before Alva left the Netherlands, recalled by the king. He was as bewildered at the lack of success of his harsh methods as at the stubbornness of the rebels.

The Beggars never had it all their own way, even at sea. The Spaniards, with larger ships and resources, could engage in counter-blockade, and before the decade was out Boisot was drowned in a vain attempt to relieve Ziericksee. The work of keeping discipline, even if of a tolerant sort, was pursued by Sonnoy and others. Whatever might be the fortunes of Philip's lieutenants on land, they could never take freedom of passage by sea for granted.

Concurrently, and long before any formal state of war came about between England and Spain, Elizabeth's maritime strength began to be felt. Francis Drake, privateer, became known and feared throughout Philip's dominions. Drake's circumnavigation, made between 1577 and 1580, brought treasure to the queen's coffers as well as new fame to the Devonshire seaman. Whatever the queen's reservations and temporisations might be, Drake and others like him knew well enough that full-scale war would sooner or later become inevitable.

Ever since 1568 when Mary, Queen of Scots, defeated in her own country, fled to England, she had become the focus of Catholic plots. Most of them included the assassination of

Elizabeth. All were backed by the power of Spain, acting in that Catholic interest to which Philip was dedicated. Considering the honourable and even considerate treatment which Mary received from Elizabeth, the hospitality was ill-repaid.

Although some of her Catholic subjects were as loyal and devoted to Elizabeth as the great mass of English Protestants, there were others. The queen's life was saved again and again, not by her own prudence for she was careless of personal danger, but by the excellence of the intelligence service at her command, of which the presiding genius was Sir Francis Walsingham. Among the more serious plots, in which the Earl of Northumberland was implicated, was that revealed by Francis Throckmorton. He was arrested in 1583, and under threat of the rack disclosed a plan of four separate landings. One was to be in Scotland, another in Ireland, and two on the English coast – one at Arundel, in Sussex, and the other in Norfolk, where 5,000 Bavarian mercenaries were to be disembarked.

As a result of Throckmorton's revelations, Mendoza, the Spanish Ambassador, was ordered to leave the country. He did so in January 1584, Walsingham taking pleasure in seeing to the matter personally. It was now only a matter of time before Elizabeth, with overwhelming proof of her fell purposes, bowed to the necessity for the execution of her prisoner. The queen wavered long and in the meanwhile much happened, including the murder at Delft of William the Silent at the hands of the Catholic youth, Balthasar Gérard.

William's great work, the Union of Utrecht, which was to last for well over two centuries, had by that time been achieved. His heir, Philip William, Count of Buren, was in Spanish hands. He remained thus until his middle age, returning to the Netherlands only to die. Louis of Nassau had already been killed in action, but fortunately for Holland William's second son Maurice proved himself to be a soldier of outstanding ability. He was appointed stadholder at the age of seventeen, and under his leadership over the next forty years some of the finest troops in Europe were trained. Justin, William's natural son by Eve Elinex (a woman of whom little is known except that she was Flemish and later became the wife of a respectable burgher called Arondeaux) was appointed Admiral of Zeeland. He was not a very gifted young man, but as the son of the 'Father of his Country', to whose memory Justin was devoted, his name could rally waverers. When the time of the armada came, it was under Justin and the flag of Orange-Nassau that Dutch captains sailed.

Justin of Nassau (1559–1631), natural son of William the Silent, Lieutenant-Admiral of Zeeland at the time of the Spanish armada   *J. A. van Ravestyn*   Rijksmuseum, Amsterdam

Five years elapsed between the time of Throckmorton's plot and Philip's 'Enterprise of England', his 'Invincible Armada'. Each of them added to the complexities of the European scene, and brought a climax nearer. An agreement between Philip and the Duke of Guise, head of the Catholic party in France, was an immediate danger-signal which drew Elizabeth closer to the Netherlanders, whom she had treated hitherto with the greatest reserve. Even now she moved with care. Although in 1585 she sent an army to the Low Countries under the command of her favourite, Robert Dudley, Earl of Leicester, she was careful to secure a lien on Brill and Flushing, of which Sir Philip Sidney was made Governor. This lien was in force for the rest of her reign and, indeed, well beyond it.

As a grandee Leicester had the necessary prestige to impress the northern provinces, but although he had the services of such men as John Norris and Francis Vere, professional soldiers of repute, the queen could not have made a worse choice than that of her favourite. Leicester knew little of war, and the continuous feasting and flattery to which he was subjected helped to add to his pride, which was excessive, and to his quarrelsome nature, which was notorious. When the States-General bestowed on him the title of governor-general, this served to gratify a vain man, but it did the Netherlanders no good and it annoyed the queen.

By the time of Leicester's advent, Alessandro Farnese, Duke of Parma, had been given charge of the Spanish and Italian forces in the Low Countries, and had begun to achieve success both as diplomatist and general. Although he thought nothing of Leicester, Parma had much respect for the fighting qualities of the English, and made a habit of enquiring their strength and disposition whenever his forces were likely to encounter them. Parma himself had small numbers of English Catholics in his army, and it was his hope that some of Leicester's officers might betray their trust. That he had reason was shown by the fact that in due course three of them did so. Sir William Stanley, Rowland York, and a Scot named Pallot surrendered key positions which they had been appointed to defend. Stanley, who had served gallantly at Zutphen, where Sir Philip Sidney received a mortal wound, did so from Catholic conviction. The others were possibly bribed. It was just such incidents which led Philip to believe that Catholics in England would be more ready to rise, in the event of an invasion backed by the pope, than was ever likely.

Parma's siege of Antwerp, then in rebel hands, was marked by an incident, sensational enough at the time, which was to have a delayed effect after the armada had sailed. An Italian engineer in Dutch service, Federigo Giambelli, launched the most destructive instrument of war as yet devised. This was a vessel crammed with explosives. It was sent against the Spanish out-works, which consisted of a bridge of boats across the Scheldt. Fire-ships had been known of old but this invention, called a 'hell burner', proved far more lethal than anything hitherto seen. It was credited with killing 1,000 men. Spanish discipline, and Parma's resolution, were equal to the menace. The bridge was repaired, and in July 1585 the city capitulated. Giambelli crossed to England, where he was believed to be planning fresh and equally diabolical methods of destruction.

Whilst it was admirable as an example of military prowess and determination on the part of Parma – the siege lasted a year – the recapture of Antwerp was an appalling blow to the prosperity of the city. Although the event seemed at first a severe setback to the Dutch cause itself, in fact the outcome proved a blessing. Not only did foreign traders transfer their interests to the ports of the north, but many local inhabitants preferred to migrate. Thus even leading Catholics such as Johan van der Veken found it profitable to take elsewhere a knowledge of some of the most advanced financial and commercial techniques in Europe. By blockading the Scheldt, the Sea Beggars made a great contribution to the rise and future prosperity of Amsterdam and Rotterdam. By his hold on the city, Parma had robbed it of much of its value.

Leicester returned from the Netherlands in 1587, unregretted, and the uncovering of what was known as the Babington plot by Walsingham led at last to the execution of Mary, Queen of Scots. Anthony Babington, one of the principals, was not 'put to the question', as the phrase was, but confessed his part without the use of torture, vainly hoping that his frankness would get him off. He revealed plans to murder not only Elizabeth, but all her ministers. 'Of your lordship,' wrote Burghley to Leicester, when the machinations had been unfolded, 'they thought rather of poisoning than of slaying.' Mary was executed for complicity on 8 February.

In the summer of 1587, Drake, in the course of an outrageously daring raid on Cadiz, 'singed the King of Spain's beard' and postponed the sailing of Philip's great fleet, destroying many small coasters carrying wood for cooperage. It was from this sortie that he wrote words, in a letter to Walsingham, which have since become well-known, not least for expressing the spirit in which

Sir Francis Drake (1540–96)
miniature by Nicholas Hilliard   NPG

he and his fellows faced a threat which was publicised throughout Europe. 'There must be a beginning of any good matter, but the continuing to the end, until it be thoroughly finished, yields the true glory. . . . God made us all thankful again and again that we have, although it be little, made a beginning on the coast of Spain.'

As if to counter-balance Drake's stroke, Parma besieged and took Sluys, which fell after a gallant defence, mainly by the English under Sir Roger Williams. Parma was becoming dove-like in his attitude to any attempt on England itself, which he had once urged, and was increasingly distracted from his main task of defeating the Dutch rebels by Philip's insistence that he move against Protestant forces in France which were a threat to his flank.

Although he had the southern districts of the Netherlands fairly well in hand, Parma's difficulties in playing his assigned part in seconding the efforts of Medina Sidonia were considerable. Handicapped by the activities of Justin's fleet, which was reinforced in the early months of 1588 by a small English squadron (with which Dutch liaison was bad), Parma spent time and employed much labour in constructing new canals. These were designed to link Sluys and Nieuport. By their means, as well as by making use of older waterways, his troops could pass from the

The fire-ship attack on the Spanish armada, 1588   *an unknown artist* NMMG

Scheldt above Antwerp to Dunkirk Haven without once venturing into open water. On Parma's estimate, if given favourable weather conditions, a flotilla could be off the North Foreland and nearing Margate, which Philip had suggested as a landing place, 'between dusk and dawn of an April night'.

Being a soldier, Parma was quick to recognise that however efficient might be his efforts in the direction of improved inland transport, none of which would be wasted even if the proposed invasion never took place, the fact of a well-armed Dutch and English presence in the open sea meant that his troops, setting out on the crossing in vulnerable craft, would need close protection from a powerful detachment from the armada itself. He wrote in this sense to the king. Such a detachment would, of course, only be possible if overwhelming success was achieved by Medina Sidonia.

It has sometimes been supposed that if the armada had been commanded by the Marquis of Santa Cruz instead of Medina Sidonia, the course of affairs would have been more favourable to the Spanish cause. This is doubtful. Santa Cruz, it is true, was the leading figure in Spanish naval history. He had been in charge of the reserve of galleys at the great battle of Lepanto in 1571, where his efforts to second Don John of Austria against the Turks played a major part in the victory. Later, after Philip had annexed

17

Portugal, Santa Cruz won successes off Terceira in the Azores against a mixed force of Portuguese and French, possibly aided by some English privateers. The events took place in 1583 and they gave the victor an inflated idea of the promise of an attempt on England. He had found that an enemy who invited or allowed himself to be boarded was likely to be an easy prey.

The marquis was due for some shocks. At the time of Terceira he was a man approaching sixty, with his more vigorous years behind him. His recent successes had been won against ill-organised people. When, four years later, he realised what Drake could do in Spanish home waters – Santa Cruz lost the galleon which was being fitted out for his flagship – he became less sanguine. Added to this, his own staff work in organising the fleet which Philip was building up for the 'enterprise' was bad. The administrative chaos which he found at Cadiz and elsewhere is said to have hastened his death, which occurred in February 1588. Whether this was so or not, his replacement by the modest, reluctant but courageous and efficient duke, inexperienced though he was at sea, was possibly no bad thing for Philip's prospects. Medina Sidonia soon had the preparations in better shape. Had Santa Cruz survived, it is likely that his career would have ended sadly.

If Giambelli's sinister contrivance was something new to war, so was the armada itself. It was the most powerful assembly of ships ever gathered at one time under sail. It amazed those who observed it from ashore. Viewed close, there seemed to be a forest of masts, and there were in fact over 130 ships of all sorts under Medina Sidonia's supreme command They carried 30,000 men, about two-thirds of them soldiers assigned to boarding duties. Soldiers also made up most of the gun crews.

The first-line strength was composed of galleons – one of the largest, built for the spice trade, being the property of the Grand Duke of Tuscany. The finest, like the *San Martin*, were Portuguese. Those of Castile comprised the 'King's Indian Guard', their normal duty being to protect the silver fleets from the mines of the New World. Four galleasses from Naples were designed to combine the advantages of oar and sail, although they had very limited success. Finally, there were forty-four converted merchantmen, some of them with temporary fighting castles fore and aft, mounting heavy guns. Well-protected by a formidable screen were the necessary store ships, some of them chartered from the

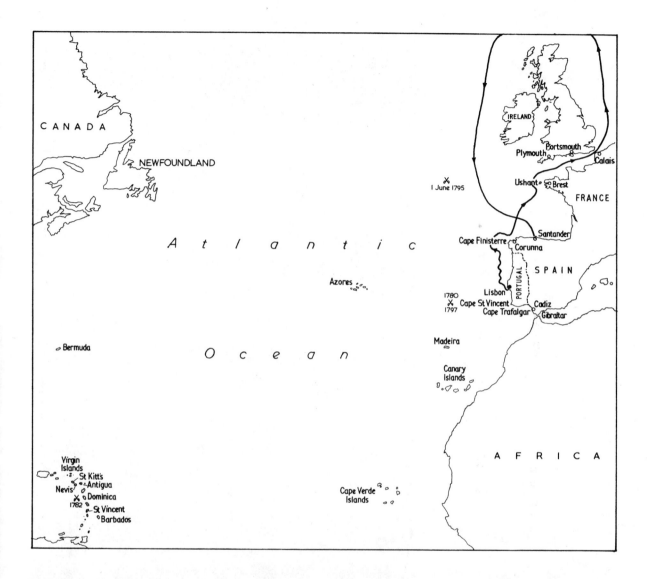

Track of the armada, and the West Indies

Hanseatic towns. They were beamy and slow. Lighter craft served as despatch vessels, some of them being detached with messages for Parma, who actually remained ignorant of the advent of the armada until it was off the Isle of Wight.

Being near their own shore, the English were not encumbered with store ships, and Lord Howard of Effingham, the Commander-in-Chief, had about eighty-four regular men-of-war or requisitioned merchantmen on which he could call during the running fight up-Channel from Plymouth. To these would be added a miscellaneous force of some forty ships under Lord Henry Seymour, when the fleet reached the Straits of Dover. Seymour's duty was to prevent a surprise landing on the coast of Kent.

Lord Howard of Effingham (1536–
1624), commander of the English
fleet against the armada
an unknown artist   NPG

The best English ships, the 'race-built' galleons with finer lines and less superstructure than those of the enemy had been built under the eye of Sir John Hawkins as Treasurer and Comptroller of the Navy. Howard's flagship, the *Ark Royal*, had been ordered as a private venture by Sir Walter Ralegh, who had at first named her after himself, but made her over to the queen. Howard reported: 'I think her the odd ship in the world for all conditions, and truly I think there can be no great ship make me change and go out of her.' The queen had granted Ralegh most of the confiscated lands of the traitor Babington. He turned the benefit to such good account that his ship survived for half a century.

Figures can mislead, but in tonnage, which was reckoned as tons burden or carrying capacity, there was not much difference between the largest ships of the two sides, which would have been rated at about 1,000 tons apiece. The English, having no soldiers aboard, depended on seamen for gun crews, and in numbers and weight of metal Spanish advantage was marked. Moreover, some of their ships were armed with 50-pounder full cannon, the English relying on a few demi-cannon and lighter-shotted culverins. Spanish powder was good, being 'fine corned' or pistol quality. Where the English scored was in the fact that their ships were handier, faster and manœuvred with freedom. Further, recent research on wrecks and recovered war material has indicated that Spanish shot was not to be compared with that supplied by the iron-masters and gun-founders of Sussex. That was why, in the clashes which occurred between the Devon coast and the roadstead off Calais, Spanish ships suffered far more severely, both in damage and casualities, than their opponents.

Wooden ships were rarely sunk by gunfire alone. Holes could be plugged and leaks stopped by competent carpenters and ship-wrights, but had the English been supplied with more plentiful ammunition, shot might have accounted for other vessels besides the *La Maria Juan* of the Squadron of Biscay, which appears to have succumbed to battering near Gravelines in the later stages of the battle.

Tactically, the Spanish object was to close and grapple, when trained soldiers would do the rest; that of the English was to keep their distance, shooting at the most effective range. Ralegh wrote a passage in his *History of the World* which for succinct summary will not be bettered.

The Spanish had an army aboard them, and he [Howard] had none: they had more ships than he had, and of higher building and charging; so that, had he entangled himself with those great and powerful vessels, he had greatly endangered this Kingdom of England. ... But our Admiral knew his advantage, and held it; which had he not done, he had not been worthy to have held his head.

According to the English calendar, which was then and indeed until 1751–2 ten days earlier than the Gregorian or new style in use on the continent, Spanish progress up-Channel continued from 19 July until Medina Sidonia brought his ships to an anchor off Calais eight days later, to find Parma unready. The armada had been attacked in various running fights, but the admiral's discipline was, by and large, as good as his dispositions, and his orders were obeyed. It is true that he had suffered three losses. The *San Salvador* had had a magazine explosion and had later been taken by the English, badly damaged. The great *Nuestro Señora del Rosario* of Andalusia, commanded by Don Pedro de Valdes, surrendered tamely to Drake after receiving some damage through collision. A hulk, the *San Pedro et Menor*, had apparently deserted. But the first-line casualties could partly be attributed to accident, and when the armada reached Calais it was virtually intact. No English ships had been sunk, or were ever to be, yet Medina Sidonia could still feel confidence in his command.

It was off Calais, during the night of 28–9 July, that Howard planned his next step. The French Governor, Gourdon, as a neutral, refused to supply munitions of war to the armada, which was getting low in ammunition; but he did a profitable trade with the duke in provisions, charging outrageous prices. Exactly thirty years earlier, Elizabeth's sister, Mary, Queen of England (who was then married to Philip of Spain) had lost the place, the name of which, so she said, would be found written on her heart. Calais was a relic of once great Anglo-French territories, and it fell during the last year of her reign. Ironically, Philip had recommended strengthening the defences, but this was not done. Medina Sidonia had no designs on the town, but it was conveniently close to Spanish-held territory, where he could hope to make some firm arrangement with Parma. Alas for both men, Parma was blockaded by Justin, and reported that it must be at least a week before his troops were ready to embark at Dunkirk. With the English undefeated and with Seymour's fresh ships joined to Howard's, the outlook was at best unpromising. Ralegh, shore duties behind him now that the West Country was no longer in danger, visited Howard on 28 July on board the *Ark Royal* with a message from the queen 'to attack the armada in some way or to engage it if he could not burn it'.

The advice was superfluous. Howard had already decided that wind and tide would serve for an attack by fire-ships. Fishing boats would have answered the purpose, and a number had actually been requisitioned at Dover by Walsingham. Howard could not wait for them so eight ships from within his own resources were prepared. Masts and rigging were thoroughly tarred; guns were left on board double-shotted, so that they went off of their own accord when the flames reached them. The ships were bigger than anything that had hitherto served the same purpose – another way in which the armada campaign was something new in naval warfare. They included the *Thomas*, of 200 tons, which belonged to Drake, and the 150 ton *Bark Bond*, which belonged to Hawkins.

Medina Sidonia was not taken by surprise. He had already warned his captains of the likelihood of such an attack. He had himself considered using fire-ships when he discovered that the English fleet was, at the outset, held in the port of Plymouth by conditions of wind favourable to the armada. Drake had met with them at Cadiz the previous summer. One of the duke's most trusted officers, Captain Serrano, was given charge of a screen of patrol boats to watch for the attempt. It would be of a sort which could often be foiled by a courageous approach, followed up by smart boat-work with grapnels and hawsers.

This time it was to be different. The fire-ships advanced in line abreast, in the charge of John Young, a Devonshire captain who was a follower of Drake. Young did not give the order to abandon his ships until the last moment, almost as the guns began to fire. The patrols managed to pull the outer ones off course, but a rumour seems to have spread round the Spanish fleet that these comparatively large vessels were not the usual fire-ship type at all, but 'hell-burners' such as Giambelli had employed at Antwerp. The siege was only three years past, and everyone had heard about the episode. It had even been depicted on one of Parma's medals, to show what he had overcome. Was not Giambelli now in England? Was this some new mischief? Giambelli was in fact engaged in trying to improve the defences of London, but no Spaniard off Calais could possibly have known that. Thus, his legend continued to help the same cause that he had already served well.

Although the fire-ships did no direct damage, drifting away shoreward and burning out on the French beaches, something like panic followed their appearance. This did not happen with the greater ships, but less experienced crews were affected. When captains cut their cables, as most of them did, the normal procedure was to buoy the severed end so that the anchorage could be found later, if and when the ship returned. In the darkness, confusion and haste, this was not done. There was also one direct casualty. The big galleass *San Lorenzo* fouled her rudder and collided with another ship. She began to draw dangerously near the French coast – then she struck.

For once, Howard's conduct was other than could have been expected. Instead of following every motion of Medina Sidonia, who was successfully making sustained efforts to rally his scattering forces, the English commander-in-chief stood away for the *San Lorenzo*, intent on a prize, or at least on loot. Sixty men were sent off in the *Ark Royal*'s longboat. After a stiff fight, in which Howard's men were joined by others, the Spanish captain, Don Hugo de Moncada, was killed and the Spaniards surrendered. Looting then began, and the boat parties might even have got the ship afloat again later had not Governor Gourdon, who had been watching the scene with mounting excitement, sent word to say that the *San Lorenzo* and her guns were French property, since she was a wreck in territorial waters.

Howard might have disputed the matter had not Gourdon reinforced his message by accurate fire from Calais Castle. The English then withdrew. But in setting about the galleass, Howard had put himself out of touch with Medina Sidonia for more than three hours. It was a bad example, and if Gourdon had not acted as he did Howard's delay might have been still longer. Drake, with his usual luck, had gathered some prize-money during the run up-Channel. Howard doubtless felt it appropriate that he should have some too.

During those hours, when the armada was off Gravelines, Medina Sidonia succeeded in forming a protective rearguard which allowed his weaker and more damaged ships a chance to get away towards the broader reaches of the North Sea. The English, with Drake prominent, repeatedly tried to break up the Spanish formations and to cut off individual ships, but the galleons stood firm in each others' support. Fighting was fierce and almost continuous. Sometimes it was at closer quarters than anything that had occurred in the Channel encounters, but Medina Sidonia's activity, leadership and skill were such that the English had no further successes.

It was otherwise with the Dutch. Captain Pedro Calderon, who had command of the large *San Salvador*, which was heavily armed and full of fight, recorded that the galleon *San Felipe*, of the Squadron of Portugal, distinguished herself particularly. She was well supported by the slightly smaller *San Mateo*. The duke

Design for tapestry celebrating the defeat of the Spanish armada, 1588 NMMG

sent a diver to try to stop some of the worst leaks in the *San Mateo*, but both she and the *San Felipe* were driven shoreward, not altogether under control, between Nieuport and Dunkirk. There they were attacked by three of Justin's blockaders. After three hours' resistance they grounded on the Flemish banks, where the battered wrecks fell into Dutch hands. Although the more vital damage had been done by English gunfire, destruction was completed by the Dutch. In view of the Spanish presence at Dunkirk, Justin's captains were skilful in rescuing their prisoners and getting them away to Flushing.

Thanks to the blockade, Medina Sidonia had no harbour on the Flemish or Dutch coasts to which he could direct his ships; and if the wind had not shifted in a way which seemed like a miracle to the harassed Spaniards, there would have been many wrecks on the banks of Zeeland.

The shift of wind, which Medina Sidonia described as 'God's mercy', enabled him to head northward, and it was clear that his best course was to return home round the north of Scotland. His ships were by now far too much damaged and too low in ammunition for any other course to be practicable. He was pursued by the English so far as their limited supplies held out.

The Spanish suffered much from wind and weather. The number of sick was growing, and in some vessels there was scarcely any water. Something like fifty ships were lost altogether, many of them on the rocks or in the bays of northern and western Ireland on the way back to Spain. Others, limping home, were too damaged to be of any further service. This was true even of the great Tuscan galleon, *Florencia*, which her owners never saw again. Casualties among the men were proportionately higher than was the case with the ships.

The armada failed, not ignominiously but completely. It had been through no lack of courage and ability on the part of its commander. He survived for many years to continue to serve his exacting king, but never again at sea. He had been foiled by tactics, determination, bad weather, and a poor over-all plan – also because Parma had been unready. Medina Sidonia deserved no reproaches, and received none.

The English had done as well as they had expected; the Dutch even better. The two galleons Justin had taken, together with 400 prisoners of war, were from the duke's own Squadron of Portugal. They were well-manned and well-defended. Justin's captains, in their small vessels, had done splendidly in making sure of their destruction. To this must be added the effect of their blockade, which, together with his own hesitations, made Parma so unusually ineffective.

At the time of the campaign, Lord Howard of Effingham knew so little of Dutch activity, since Anglo-Dutch liaison continued to be bad, that he actually reported: 'There is not a Hollander or Zeelander at sea.' Such lack of information was not the admiral's fault, and he was later to atone for his statement in a remarkable way. He sent for Hendrik Vroom, a Dutch artist born at Haarlem and twenty years old when the fighting took place, to employ his services as a recorder. Vroom, a pupil of Pieter Brueghel the Elder, was a tapestry designer and Howard commissioned him to execute a series representing the defeat of the armada by the English fleet, to decorate the House of Lords.

The tapestries survived until 1834, when the old House of Lords was burnt down, the only remaining record being a series of engravings made in the eighteenth century by John Pine. Howard, although making sure that Vroom immortalised the deeds of the fleet commanded by himself, was thus the means of introducing an important Dutch marine artist to this country. The admiral was the first of many similar patrons, and the effect of his choice was to stimulate a native school which in course of time produced valuable work. The gesture was at least a tribute to Dutch skill from the right quarter. The Dutch had in fact played an important part at the time of the armada, and they were right to be proud of it. Vroom could have recorded their own share, had he found such a patron as Howard among his compatriots.

2 Tromp and Blake

Justin of Nassau has his place in a line which came to include some very notable leaders, of whom the best known were to be Maarten Tromp and Michael de Ruyter. Tromp's later career brought him into conflict with the most gifted English commander at sea since the time of Elizabeth, the Parliamentary colonel-turned-admiral, Robert Blake. How the two men came to serve against each other is a complex story, the outline of which needs to be followed if a rivalry leading to three stubborn wars is to be understood.

For the Dutch the armada was a comparatively minor episode, marginally affecting their own protracted and agonised struggle with Spain, which had begun soon after the accession of Philip II as ruler over the seventeen provinces of the Netherlands in 1553. There followed the savagery of Alva's regime as Philip's lieutenant; the Union of Utrecht, covering the seven northern provinces, which was the crowning work of William the Silent's resistance; the military achievements of Maurice of Nassau, followed by a truce which lasted from 1609 until war was resumed in 1621. Maurice's brother, Frederick Henry, succeeded as stadholder in 1625 and showed much skill in the field during the twenty years in which he held office.

At sea, the Dutch enjoyed three exceptional successes, as well as many lesser ones. In 1607 Jacob van Heemskerk won a victory off Gibraltar in which a Spanish flagship was destroyed, and where Tromp, whose father commanded a frigate, had his first taste of action at the age of nine. In 1628 Piet Hein became a national hero after he had captured the Spanish Silver Fleet off the coast of Cuba, to return with treasure amounting to fifteen million florins. The third event occurred eleven years later, when Tromp – by then a seasoned campaigner – annihilated a Spanish fleet in the Downs, within sight of the coast of Kent, and an English squadron.

Frederick Henry died in 1647. He was succeeded by his son, William II, as stadholder of five provinces, and it was during William's brief period of office that Spain at last recognised Dutch independence at the Treaty of Munster, one of the landmarks in European history. William had married Mary, Princess Royal of England, the eldest daughter of Charles I and Henrietta Maria, a girl celebrated for her beauty and intelligence. William's sudden and early death in 1650, followed by the birth of a posthumous son, later to become William III and a future King of England, was inevitably succeeded by a period in which the House of Orange suffered eclipse. It was during this so-called stadholder-less phase, which lasted until William III was of an age to exercise authority, that the Nassau emblem temporarily disappeared from the tricolour worn by Dutch ships of war.

While it is true to say that Dutch independence arose from the use of sea power, and could not have been gained without it, the fact repays examination. Geographically the United Provinces, small in area besides their easterly neighbours and less extensive than the southern provinces, are made up of islands and inlets, an almost enclosed sea in the Zuider, rich agricultural land, and waterways in which as much use as possible is made of fresh-water canals. These supplement the wider river navigations.

The prime advantage in earlier days was mobility. Even the most soil-bound farmer could, if need be, take to the water. Once afloat he and his portable possessions were far safer from rapine and from legitimate state regulation and taxation than those of a land-bound creature. Out of a population of perhaps $1\frac{1}{2}$ million at the end of the sixteenth century, a far higher proportion than in any other area except Venice drew their subsistence, accumulated their wealth, and found some measure of safety by way of ship-borne traffic. And in an era when road transport was conditioned by surfaces which were often impassable in winter and at best were indifferent, the canal boat and the ship, dependent though they were on manual strength and the vagaries of the wind, were almost express in speed and ability to convey a quantity and variety of goods which would have entailed massive organisation and serious risk overland. There is no more impressive instance in the history of Europe, again except for the Republic of Venice, of feats which could be achieved through the craft of the ship and the boatwright than was shown by the Dutch in the days when they were at last beginning to perceive and extend their own power.

Knowledge that the sea was pre-eminently their salvation and their opportunity had long been realised in Holland and Zeeland. The germ of Dutch expansion as a seafaring people may be seen in what came to be known as the Great Fishery. Early in the fifteenth century a change in the habits of the Gulf Stream caused huge shoals of herring to migrate from the Baltic to the North Sea. The Dutch were ready to exploit this source of profit. Efficient methods of salting and curing, applied first by a Zeelander called Beukels (to whom his compatriots should have put up a golden statue), were applied on an ever more extensive scale. Supplies of salt drawn from the Bay of Bourgneuf, on the Biscay shore of France, or from Setúbal, in Portugal, sometimes became insufficient or for political reasons impossible to obtain, and this caused Dutch venturers to find a valuable new source of the commodity across the Atlantic in Venezuela. This was an instance of how necessity – as well as a thirst for riches or adventure – has sometimes been the mother of exploration as well as of invention.

The Fishery soon came to be established on a regular basis, with a well-established routine which did not vary from year to year. Not content with coastal fishing the Dutch sailed in their *buizen*, or 'busses' as the English called them. They started in Shetland on 24 June, St John's Day, fished their way south, often close to the Scottish and English coasts, until they reached the Thames estuary about the beginning of December. Compared with English fishing craft, Dutch boats were advanced in design – they were decked, they carried salt on board, and they were able to wait for bigger catches, while remaining economical to operate. They could even transfer barrelled fish to attendant ships which carried the catch to harbour, leaving the busses to continue work. The whole business was organised by what was called the 'College of the Fishery', and was based mainly on the ports at the mouth of the Meuse.

If the herring industry, which, by the start of the seventeenth century regularly employed more than 500 vessels, was a sure source of employment and prosperity (since the salted or smoked product found a ready market throughout Europe, particularly in the Catholic countries), there were others of importance. There was, for example, the cod fishery of the Dutch coast and the Dogger Bank, and Arctic whaling, with a 'factory' on the shores of Spitzbergen to process the huge carcasses and extract the valuable oil. A contemporary reckoned that these fisheries were as lucrative as the silver mines which the Spaniards were exploiting in Peru, and the profits were put to better use. Fishing being seasonal, ships could be released for other uses during the close season.

This made the larger of them available for the Dutch carrying trade, which grew to be world-wide after the Portuguese discovered an African route to the Far East. First in importance was the 'mother trade', as it was called, in which corn was taken all

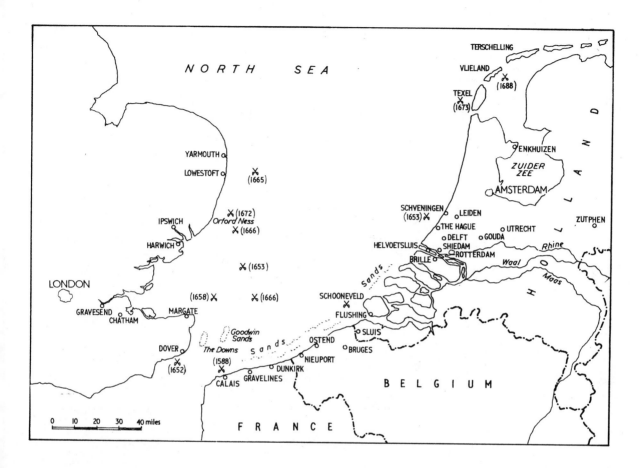

over Europe from Danzig, by way of the Sound. In 1618 over 1,700 Dutch ships paid Sound dues at Helsingør (Elsinore), as against only 90 English. Even seventy years later, by which time English expansion had become considerable, the Dutch still sent four times as many vessels past Helsingør as their chief rivals.

Dutch shipbuilders, the most advanced in Europe, were the first to employ wind-driven sawmills, which helped to reduce the price of the products of their yards and led to orders from all over the continent. The *fluyt*, a type constantly under scrutiny for ways to improve its capacity, soon became almost standardised, being recognised as unsurpassed as a general-purpose cargo carrier. The length was from four to six times the beam, masts were stepped so as to allow as large a hold as possible, they were of shallow draught, and internal dimensions were designed to take every legitimate advantage of whatever regulations happened to be in force at Helsingør, where the Danish kings exacted toll from all foreign ships making use of the best passage in the Baltic.

To crown the rest, the foundation in 1602 of a Dutch East

Indies Company, followed less than twenty years later by a West India Company, showed that the seamen of the United Provinces, long before political independence had been accorded to their country, considered the entire world a legitimate scene for their activity.

Maarten Tromp was born at Brill in 1597, two years earlier than Blake, and was typical of many Dutchmen bred to the sea. His father had been as at home on board a merchantman as a ship of war, and Maarten was familiar with salt-water before he could toddle. His career covered some of the tensest years of the struggle with Spain, and he never had cause to feel affection for England, for when he was twelve he saw his father killed in action with an English interloper off the coast of Guinea. He learnt English the hard way, during two years servitude as a cabin-boy. After he returned home he joined the merchant service, and when still in his early twenties he was once more made prisoner, this time by a Barbary pirate, and spent a year in captivity.

Tromp rejoined the naval service in 1622, and he never looked back. He was soon given command of a frigate, the type of vessel in which his father had made his name. Later he became flag captain to the great Piet Hein, who was killed in a fight with pirates from Ostend soon after his return from Cuba.

Tromp's first major exploit as a naval commander was when, in charge of 11 ships and flying his flag as Lieutenant-Admiral of Holland, he surprised a Spanish squadron near Gravelines in February 1639, completely destroyed it, and then proceeded to blockade Dunkirk, whence the enemy had come. The Battle of the Downs was the direct consequence of the Spanish effort to raise the blockade. They considered this matter to be of such importance that they sent Admiral d'Oquendo, whose father had gallantly commanded the Squadron of Guipuzcoa with the armada, with a strong fleet to relieve it.

With a total force not much less than that of the armada of 1588, d'Oquendo was ordered to convey 24,000 troops in fifty transports, nine of which were hired from England. This was not merely to relieve Dunkirk but to reinforce the Spanish army in the Netherlands, which was engaged with the French as well as the Dutch.

As in the time of Philip II, Spanish planning took too much for granted. It assumed that, in spite of the French, d'Oquendo would have a clear run up-Channel, and that as he was in overwhelming

Lieutenant-Admiral Maarten Tromp
(1597–1653)   *after Jan Livensz*
NMMG

numerical strength, he would be able to brush aside Tromp's blockaders. He could have been certain that Tromp would not be taken by surprise. The Dutch had scouts constantly on the look-out between Dunkirk and the western approaches to the Channel. On 16 September, fifty-one years since Philip II's fleet had been sighted off the Cornish coast, d'Oquendo was said to be near Selsey Bill. His fleet appeared to be ordered with something of the precision which had been a predominant feature of Medina Sidonia's discipline.

Tromp had not a tithe of the resources which had been at the disposal of Lord Howard in the earlier campaign, yet experience led him to believe that attack was the right policy. Although he had only seventeen ships with him at the outset, he did not hesitate. At first d'Oquendo stood up boldly as Tromp advanced in his flagship, the *Amelia*, and at one stage the Dutch were almost encircled near the mouth of the Somme. But the *Santiago*, d'Oquendo's flagship, received severe damage when the Spaniards tried to close. He himself had given no tactical instructions to his captains, apart from ordering them to maintain formation, and when the wind changed he tamely retreated across the Channel, seeking refuge in the Downs, near Dover, realising that he had no chance of reaching Dunkirk without fighting a major battle.

In England the court was for Spain, the people for the Dutch. The situation prompted Charles I to offer help to the highest bidder. He would protect the Spanish fleet with a squadron of his own for a consideration of £150,000; or he would stand aside and allow Tromp to have his way, if his French allies would consent to use the army which was in their pay in Germany to help restore his nephew, the King of Bohemia, to his possessions in the Palatinate.

d'Oquendo was allowed to send ashore for water and supplies, for which, following the example of M. Gourdon of Calais at the time of the armada, they were charged outrageous prices, but no warlike stores changed hands.

Tromp was presently joined by seventeen more ships, but even so d'Oquendo still had great superiority. Having paused to consider and to revictual he should have pushed on, according to his orders from home, for while Tromp could look for reinforcements, he could not.

Weeks passed, and d'Oquendo did nothing. The Spanish soldiers were removed out of the nine English transports, and one or two of the others managed to steal away by night, evading the Dutch. But the main fleet did not move, even when Tromp offered d'Oquendo a gift of 500 barrels of gunpowder to fight it out. Urgent messages to the five admiralities of the United Provinces and to the Prince of Orange to strain every nerve to send him as many ships as possible, resulted in prodigies of exertion. Work went on night and day in all the dockyards of Holland, and in less than a month Tromp had been reinforced in such good measure that he found himself in command of over a hundred sail, including fire-ships. For the most part they were smaller than d'Oquendo's ships, but size in itself was nothing. Tromp believed that he had more than enough resources for a battle of annihilation. So confident was he that he told an Englishman that King Charles would soon have the Spaniards' guns, his countrymen their ships, and the devil their men.

This proved no boast. On 21 October, at a season when decisive action could not be delayed much longer owing to the approach of winter, Tromp detached Admiral Witte de With for special duties. He was given a force of thirty ships and told to watch the actions of Sir John Pennington, who was in command of the

English squadron, and not to allow him to interfere. He himself then bore down upon the Spanish fleet, the Dutch tricolour flying at his main top-masthead.

Seldom has a victory been more complete. d'Oquendo and his Spaniards fought stubbornly, as was their way, but their admiral had no idea how to conduct a naval action, no tactical plan. Almost his whole force was destroyed, run ashore, or captured. Some 7,000 men are known to have perished, many of them in the galleon *Santa Theresa* which was set on fire. Dutch losses were trifling, a mere handful of killed and wounded. Tromp himself engaged the Spanish flagship, which d'Oquendo managed to save. He was fortunate to escape under cover of mist, with 1,700 shot holes in the ship's sides.

Tromp's final gesture must have given him much satisfaction. After his triumphant violation of English territorial waters, he added to the indignity suffered by the English king by lowering his flag, in mock acknowledgement of Charles's claim to sovereignty in the Narrow Seas.

Tromp's attitude towards the English was tinged with bitterness arising from personal experience, and he had little but contempt for the Spaniards as seamen. No one could fail to respect the

The Battle of the Downs, 1639
an unknown Dutch artist   NMMG

qualities of Spanish soldiers, who were among the best infantry in Europe. At sea, it was otherwise. Both Dutch and English took Spanish bravery for granted, and Spanish ship-building often proved notable, yet Spain could rarely produce that blend of seamanship and tactical skill which fellow-sailors could regard as fully professional. A man like Tromp, thoroughly knowledgeable in nautical matters, treated d'Oquendo with contempt because he despised a man, however brave, who could not think and plan on behalf of his captains and his fleet. It is true that his attitude towards the English at the time of the Battle of the Downs was not markedly different, but it changed when at last he faced an opponent as formidable as Blake.

Nearly two years after the Battle of the Downs, the marriage took place of Charles's daughter to William, the heir of Frederick Henry of Orange. The event seemed a promising landmark in Anglo-Dutch relations, as indeed it proved, although not until a later generation. In England, the advent of civil war was soon to absorb so much of the nation's energies and resources that foreign affairs had of necessity to take a second place. The inevitable disruption of trade, together with a continuation of the struggle between France and Spain, served as an opportunity for the Dutch to increase their strong position at sea.

Charles had not neglected the navy. His demand for ship money had been one of the causes of his troubles. He also built the finest ship of her time, naming her *Sovereign of the Seas* to emphasise claims not only in home waters but well outside their limits. This ship was supervised by the monarch at every stage, and she was a forerunner of the three-decked line-of-battleship which was to become the ultimate in majestic power throughout the later era of sail. Yet almost as soon as war opened, parliament achieved command of the sea and held it. It was not absolute; and it led to no important actions, but it helped towards Charles's defeat.

At first, Dutch opinion on English affairs was divided. The Orange party gave what aid it could to the king, but the States-General were hostile to his cause, more particularly to his claim to powers at sea which, if pressed, would have seriously affected the Great Fishery. The Orange influence was strong enough to silence protest against the supply of munitions to the Royalists, and an embassy from Holland even tried mediation, the sole result of which was to arouse suspicions as to Dutch neutrality. Help to the king continued long after his cause was hopeless.

Royalist ships were allowed to refit in Dutch harbours, and in July 1648, when matters had become desperate, the young Prince of Wales, who was at Helvoetsluys, actually made an attempt on shipping in the Thames estuary – rather in the manner, though without a fraction of the skill, which was to be shown by de Ruyter nearly twenty years later when the English and Dutch were at war. When his provisions ran out, the prince had to return to Holland.

The realisation that Cromwell and the army intended to bring Charles I to trial led all parties in the United Netherlands to combine in an embassy to London to plead for mercy towards him. It met with no more success than had attended the earlier attempt at intervention.

When Charles was executed in January 1649, the axe sent a a wave of horror through Europe. The Dutch at first refused to recognise the Commonwealth, and in France an English merchant at Nantes begged a correspondent not to address him as *Anglais*, for, he said, the nation was so much hated that he could not pass through the streets in safety. The way of the pioneer is apt to be dangerous, and it was not until the following century that France herself followed England's example.

With extreme lack of tact, the Commonwealth chose the Dutch-born Isaac Dorislaus as its emissary to the Hague. This was at a time when the exiled young king was himself living there, and it can have surprised no one when Dorislaus, who had prepared the formal charge of treason against Charles I, was murdered by a party of English Royalists at the inn where he had insisted on staying in spite of the advice of Walter Strickland, the regular English representative. Although the Dutch authorities tendered a formal apology, no serious attempt was made to apprehend the culprits.

The following year, when Charles II was invited to accept the crown of Scotland, he was conveyed from Holland in a frigate commanded by Cornelius Tromp, the second son of the Lieutenant-Admiral, escorted by two men-of-war supplied by the Orange party. Charles had a stormy and protracted voyage to Cromarty, and little luck after he had arrived. His adherents were beaten by Cromwell's army first at Dunbar and later at Worcester, and Charles was driven first into hiding and then into longer-lasting exile.

In certain respects Cromwell was old-fashioned, even Elizabethan in his outlook. He was of the opinion, which was naïve in the European climate of his time, that Protestant states should unite, and this despite sharp experiences of the clouded atmosphere which could prevail between religious sections even within his own country. He was determined to make every effort not only to be friendly with the Dutch, but to ally himself with them. He even proposed political fusion, and was pained when Strickland and Oliver St John, sent to Holland to negotiate, were greeted in public with shouts of 'king murderers'. A refusal by the Dutch to consider measures against refugees helped by the recently widowed Mary of Orange, now the mother of an infant son, was perhaps to have been expected. The States-General would have been glad of a commercial treaty on terms of equality, but they were unwilling to go further towards political union than an agreement that each country would assist the other by arms, provided that the country needing help paid for it!

Exasperation in London led to the passing of a Navigation Act in October 1651 which was aimed at the Dutch carrying trade, a continual source of envy. This measure forbade the importation of the produce of Asia, Africa and America except in English ships or those belonging to the plantations overseas. It also required that the majority of the crews should be subjects of the Commonwealth. Goods from a European country should be imported only in ships owned by Englishmen or the people of the exporting country.

It was long held that this act was a main cause of the war with Holland which broke out in the following year. In so far as principle was concerned, this was true; but the act could not have been strictly enforced, for the sufficient reason that there was not enough available English shipping or sailors to meet the country's needs. Owing to the Civil War, the navy was strong; less so, the merchant fleet. Other causes were the English claim to a right of search. Since the Dutch were determined to maintain what they called the freedom of the seas, they were prepared to fight to assert the doctrine that the flag covers the goods. They issued orders to Tromp, their Lieutenant-Admiral, to resist all efforts to visit Dutch ships, in particular those carrying material to the French, who were then engaged in an unofficial maritime war with the English. Finally, Dutch reluctance to strike their flag in acknowledgement of what the English considered to be their sovereignty in the Narrow Seas continued to be a source of trouble. Summing everything up, there was much in an English merchant's remark, 'the trade of the world is too little for us both, therefore one must down'.

The Dutch were reluctant to go to war. They had much to lose; and after a first encounter off Dover in May 1652 between Blake and Tromp, when Tromp, who was protecting a convoy,

returned to the French coast with the loss of two ships, the States-General agreed to regard the affair as an accident. Tromp was even required to strike the flag when necessary, and only to resist search if attacked. But the Commonwealth Government remained intransigent, and so, having no choice, the States-General in July ordered their admiral to lose no chance to attack the English fleet and 'to do all imaginable damage to it'. The decision caused heavy hearts. Adriaan Paw, the venerable Grand Pensionary, who had been in London attempting a last-minute settlement, sadly remarked that 'the English are about to attack a mountain of gold; we are about to attack a mountain of iron'.

The 'mountain of iron' possessed a good navy, and had seasoned officers to lead it. Blake and Tromp had met at least once before, off the Isles of Scilly when Blake was conducting an intricate campaign against a small but determined Royalist fleet. Campaigning led him as far afield as the Mediterranean, and it had been concluded successfully. Tromp had been off Scilly, not, as the English Government feared, to seize the islands, but to obtain restitution for the loss of ships.

Blake's earliest sea experience is not known with any certainty,

The Dutch herring fleet guarded by a man-of-war   *A. van Salm*
NMMG

39

Robert Blake (1599–1657)
a contemporary miniature   NMMG

but he came of a ship-owning West Country family; and of his nautical ability there was never any question. He had done well as a soldier of Parliament during the Civil War, and when a trusted commander was required to take charge of affairs at sea against a new enemy there was no one better qualified. Two others, some years his junior, were later joined with him in principal command. One was George Monck, hitherto a soldier and a professional in the fullest sense of the term. The other was Richard Deane, an expert artilleryman with previous sea service.

The English had two great advantages. One was geographical. The country's position athwart the main sea route to the Dutch ports meant that the enemy would have to devote much of his strength to protecting the merchant fleets which were the source of his wealth. If the Channel was considered too dangerous, it entailed a long, time-consuming and expensive haul round the north of Scotland. Once the main part of the voyage was completed, an alliance with Denmark (which, since the Middle Ages, had included Norway) ensured some degree of protection if the ships kept to the easterly side of the North Sea. There was also the Fishery, much of which was bound to be at the mercy of the English since there was insufficient force to protect both this and the carrying trade adequately. England's other advantage was that she had less to distract her from attempting to defeat the Dutch fleet, after which convoys would be at her mercy. It is true that both sides suffered from scares of invasion. English alarm, though unjustified in the event except for small-scale raids, was the more reasonable since the hazards presented by the shallows of the Dutch coast were notorious.

It is a measure of Tromp's stature that, faced with problems which no amount of ingenuity or forethought could have overcome, he was of the opinion that Dutch policy should be aggressive. This was a view which needed courage to voice, so sensitive were mercantile interests. But it was one in which he never wavered, and he was prepared to run the risk of loss of merchant shipping from detached English squadrons in order to achieve it. Michael de Ruyter, by far the ablest of Tromp's subordinates, and a man who shared Tromp's gift of inspiring the affection of Dutch sailors – both men were known as *bestevaer* (grandad) – was in this respect in full accord with the lieutenant-admiral.

England had 85 first-line ships of war available at the outset, nearly half of which were less than 5 years old and some of very recent construction. On an average they were bigger than those of the Dutch, carried more men and heavier guns. The Elizabethan custom of hiring and adapting merchantmen to supplement the fleet was less often resorted to. Specialised ships of war, carrying out systematised tactics, was the pattern of the future.

In numbers, Holland started off at an advantage. Tromp's fleet totalled 112. Although this was only half the authorised establishment, it was a good deal more than Blake had, and the proportion of Dutch seamen accustomed to deep-sea voyaging and the handling of larger types of ship was higher than in the English fleet. One of Tromp's disadvantages was that he had to deal with five separate admiralties, those of Zeeland, South

Lieutenant-Admiral Michael de
Ruyter (1607–76), greatest of all
Dutch sea commanders
Hendrick Berckman   NMMG

The English ship *Triumph* during the
First Dutch War. She was in service
from 1623 to 1688 and had many
battle honours   *Willem van de
Velde the Younger*   NMMG

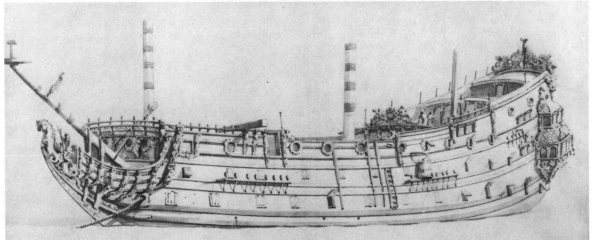

Holland, North Holland, West Friesland and Friesland. They were not noted for acting in harmony, and only dire emergencies hastened their decisions. Tromp's heartfelt complaint that after hazarding his life and doing his utmost on behalf of his country he was liable to be 'molested with subtle questions' from people ignorant of the difficulties of a commander on active service, has been echoed by admirals ever since. Also strong Orangist and anti-Orangist factions were growing in the Dutch fleet. A captured Dutch skipper remarked that while the English had chosen Blake, whom everyone could respect, the Dutch had 'purged' some of their ablest captains for political reasons. Acting as he did under Cromwell, who understood war, Blake was certainly less harassed than Tromp. 'You must handle the reins as you shall find the opportunity', wrote the Protector, 'and the ability of the fleet to be.' These were the words of a practical strategist.

Blake's orders were to watch for the Dutch East India fleet homeward bound, which offered the greatest prize to be expected. He was also to 'interrupt and disturb' the Fishery 'upon the Coast of Scotland and England', and to intercept the 'Eastland trade' – the 'mother trade' with the Baltic – being careful in so doing to 'respect and preserve' English shipping in the same area.

Tromp, seeking battle with the main English fleet, entered the Downs on 20 July and there found not Blake but Sir George Ayscue, who had twenty-one ships with him. The wind dropped and Tromp, looking for bigger game, sailed northwards when conditions allowed. By 4 August he was at anchor off Fair Isle, between Orkney and Shetland, within sight of Blake. The latter had already scattered the fishing fleet and captured half the warships guarding it. Then one of the storms which occur in northern waters blew up, preventing a general action. In the midst of the confusion, the Dutch East Indiamen arrived, together with a number of ships from the West Indies. They were eventually shepherded to home ports by Tromp.

Neither he nor Blake were satisfied with the result of the initial moves. Blake had disrupted the Fishery, but had not captured the Indiamen. Tromp had lost the chance of annihilating Ayscue, who had been in greatly inferior numbers, in order to go after Blake. He had been frustrated in his hope of giving battle by weather, shortage of supplies, the need to protect the merchantmen, and panic messages from Zeeland urging his return because it was believed that an English invasion was imminent. Nevertheless, he had ensured the safety of the merchant fleets, and his temporary suspension, at this early stage of the war, besides being offensive to his sailors, was a grave misjudgement. The officer who supplanted him, Witte de With, was disliked by Tromp's partisans, though he helped to safeguard the homecoming of the Silver Fleet (said to contain 15 million guilders in bullion, upon which trade with the Far East depended) after an inconclusive fight near Plymouth between Ayscue and de Ruyter.

Early in October, when Michael de Ruyter joined de With, their intention was to attack Blake who was in the Downs. Once again, weather led to confusion. Blake slipped away from a position of tactical disadvantage, and the encounter took place near the Kentish Knock in the Thames estuary. Blake had superior numbers, took the offensive, and got much the better of his opponents. Anxious though he had been for a decision, de Ruyter on this occasion counselled prudence, and the much-battered Dutch fleet retired to its home ports. The admirals faced some mutinous behaviour. Several Dutch captains held back, and the crew of Tromp's old flagship flatly refused to allow de With on board.

Tromp was reinstated within a few weeks, and was charged with the escort of a large fleet of merchantmen destined for the Ile de Ré, opposite La Rochelle on the Atlantic coast of France. He was to return with another fleet, homeward bound, which was to assemble at the island, the French being benevolently neutral. The problems involved in combining escort duties with aggression were made clear in a despatch from Tromp to the States-General on 6 December. Nevertheless, undaunted as ever, he applied himself so well to his task that he succeeded not only in his main object but in defeating Blake off Dungeness, He captured two English ships and sank three others, his victory being so decisive that for three months he was supreme in the Channel.

Blake, who had been disappointed in the conduct of some of his captains when faced with odds, asked to be relieved as a result of his setback, 'so that I may spend the remainder of my days in private retirement, and prayers for a blessing upon the Nation'. He made his request confidently since he knew of the appointments of Monck and Deane to the fleet, 'two such able gentlemen for the undertaking', as he described them. They were due to join shortly. For his part, Cromwell made no such mistake as had the Dutch over Tromp. His belief in Blake remained unshaken.

How justified was such trust was shown in the course of a three-day battle which took place between 28 February and 2 March 1653. By that time Monck and Deane were with Blake, and so was William Penn as Vice-Admiral. The task of the English was to intercept a fleet of equal strength to their own, under Tromp, which was bound up-Channel bringing home a

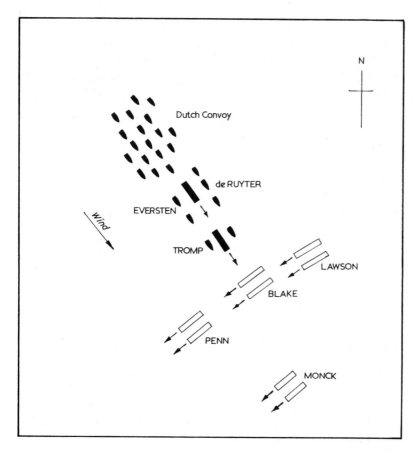

convoy of over 130 ships. Tromp had de Ruyter with him.

Contact was made off Portland Bill, and a running fight followed. Tromp had poor support from several ships, and there was a shortage of ammunition. Nevertheless, his initial attack disconcerted Blake. Several English ships were badly damaged, and Blake himself was wounded in the thigh. The first day's fighting ended about 4 pm, when the winter light was fading. During the night Tromp rejoined the convoy, which had progressed steadily towards home while the cannonade was going on. He took up a disposition in its wake, forming a strong rearguard. For the next two days Blake pursued, and there were many partial engagements. The crisis came on the third day, when the Dutch were low in powder and the convoy had fallen into some confusion. Blake gradually overcame the Dutch rearguard and made a number of prizes. Only Tromp's consummate skill prevented complete disaster. In the evening, with the wind at the north-west, Tromp found himself approaching Cap Gris Nez. It was a lee shore, with the enemy to windward. Certain that he was trapped, Blake did not press home his attack and came to anchor at nightfall. But during the hours of darkness Tromp weathered the headland. Morning found his fleet, and the greater part of the convoy, within easy distance of Gravelines. The Dutch had lost 12 ships of war and over 30 merchantmen. The battle was a turning-point of the war. Tromp came to the conclusion that the only wise policy was for merchantmen to stay in port until he had managed to inflict a crushing defeat on the English. The policy of general cover, as then adopted, was beyond the powers of his fleet.

One gleam of hope remained. This was an attack on the Newcastle colliers, on whose regular sailing London depended. By April 1653 the price of coal had risen from £2 to £5 per chaldron, and there was little to be had. Industries like brewing were idle, and there was much distress. But the colliers escaped an attack by de With, and their safe arrival in the Thames restored the situation.

As the Channel route was now an unacceptable risk, Tromp did what he could, which was to ensure that convoys which attempted the voyage north-about were safeguarded, and never gave up hope that he would defeat Blake in a major battle. The fleets cruised for more than a week in the summer of 1653 and met on 11 June near the Gabbard Shoal, about fifty miles east of Harwich. Thanks to Deane's training of the English gunners, the Dutch were smothered by heavier fire-power, and Tromp was forced to retreat behind the Dutch sandbanks with 6 ships destroyed, 11 others made prize, 800 killed, and over 1,300 prisoners.

The English had 12 ships disabled and 126 men killed. Among them was Richard Deane, who died at Monck's side from wounds from a chain-shot. Monck threw his coat over the body, then ordered it to be taken below so that the crew should not be discouraged. The action was the prelude to a blockade of the United Netherlands which was to continue for the rest of the year. News of the Dutch defeat sent corn prices to famine heights, and the stoppage of the Great Fishery left the market stalls empty of the herrings which, with bread, formed the staple diet of poorer people in Holland.

The battle of the Gabbard was important not only in the Dutch war but in the evolution of naval tactics, for it was the first occasion on which the English captains acted under regular instructions. A fortnight before the action a document had been issued over the signatures of Blake, Deane and Monck, entitled *Instructions for the Better Ordering of the Fleet in Fighting*. It was ordained that:

. . . as soon as they shall see the General engage, or make a signal by shooting off two guns and putting a red flag over the fore topmast-head, then each Squadron shall take the best advantage they can to engage the enemy next to them; and in order thereto all the ships of every Squadron shall endeavour to keep in line with the Chief unless the Chief be maimed or otherwise disabled (which God forbid).

In the same *Instructions* it was indicated that the 'line' should normally be a line ahead, by which the best use could be made of broadside gunfire. From these *Instructions* were derived a long succession of standing orders for the conduct of fleets in battle.

Being a great commander, Tromp wasted no time in blank despair or inactivity but set to work repairing his ships and reinforcing his fleet. By the beginning of August 1653 he felt ready for another sortie. His first problem was to join forces with the squadron commanded by de With, which lay at the Texel. The junction was made, but it brought on a fierce battle in which Tromp was killed. He was pierced through the breast by a shot fired, ironically enough, from a captured Dutch ship, the *Tulip*. It had been pressed into service by Monck, who, in the absence of Blake through sickness, had command of the English fleet. Tromp was carried below to a cabin, his officers standing around his death-bed. 'I have finished my course,' were his last words. 'Have good courage.'

Tromp was spared the humiliation of seeing his fleet put to flight, with great loss in ships and men. In his turn, Monck lost the *Oak* and the *Hunter*, but recaptured two ships, the *Garland* and the *Bonaventure*, taken at Dungeness. Both were so much damaged that they had to be burnt.

Monck remarked that it was as well that the Dutch had come out when they did, for he was low in stores and his men were weary with blockading. When he returned home to refit, it gave de With the chance of running a convoy north-about. The move was successful: nonetheless, de With realised that the situation was hopeless. In an outburst to the States-General he exclaimed: 'Why should I keep silence any longer? I am before my Sovereigns. I am free to speak, and I say that the English are at present masters both of us and of the seas.'

A mission arrived in London to discuss terms of peace, and Cromwell, walking in St James's Park with the Dutch deputies, observed that the interests of both nations consisted in the welfare of commerce and navigation. The universe, he thought, was wide enough for both, and if the two countries could thoroughly understand one another, they could become the leading markets to which all nations would resort.

Negotiations continued from September 1653 until the following April, and the resulting Treaty of Westminster was statesman-like in its provisions. No political alliance or entanglement was demanded of the Dutch. Nothing was said about the Fishery which might affect the matter of licences, which the English had at one time insisted on. What was included about visit and search on the high seas was put into language suitably ambiguous. English pretensions to maritime 'sovereignty' were not emphasised, but the Dutch acknowledged the propriety of saluting the English flag in home waters. They also granted compensation for losses which Englishmen had suffered in the Far East and elsewhere, particularly those which had followed a massacre at Amboyna. A further treaty was concluded with Denmark. This put the English on an equal footing with the Dutch, an important concession in view of the growing trade with the Baltic countries.

After the return of his flagship from the battle of the Texel, Tromp's body had been taken to Delft, where it was buried with all honour. A monument was placed to his memory in the Oude Kerk, where it stands with those to Princes of Orange.

Blake, recovered from his sickness, continued his career at sea against the enemies of his country, his greatest feat being the destruction of a Spanish fleet at Santa Cruz, Tenerife, in 1657. He died of fever off Plymouth on his way back to England, and was interred with great ceremony in Westminster Abbey. He was not long undisturbed. After the restoration of the monarchy his body was removed, together with that of Deane and others, and thrown into a common pit. Within our own time, a tablet has been placed in the building where he once lay to commemorate one of the ablest admirals of his own or any other age. He and Tromp were opponents worthy of one another.

Clarendon, a Royalist, wrote a memorable tribute to Blake in his history of the Civil War.

He was the first that infused that proportion of courage into the seamen by making them see by experience what mighty things they could do if they were resolved, and taught them to fight in fire as well as upon water, and though he hath been well imitated and followed, he was the first that gave the example of that kind of naval courage and bold and resolute achievements.

3 The Struggle for the Sound

There was to be no respite for the Dutch, if, after recovering from war with England, they were to retain and expand the markets they had created. Despite the Treaty of Westminster, England would continue to be a threat, but the fleet which Tromp had commanded so ably was soon to be employed with high purpose not in the Channel or North Sea, but in the confined waters of the Baltic. The 'mother trade' was seen to be endangered. At all costs it must be safeguarded; and in this respect, if in no other, the interests of England and the United Provinces coincided.

One of the main reasons concerned timber. The Dutch, having no forests of their own, relied upon imports. England, endowed with a wealth of native oak which shipwrights considered incomparable for hulls, had for centuries been prodigal with her resources, had mismanaged her forests and woodlands, so that even at the time of the armada her seamen had been glad to take in prize cargoes of timber suitable for naval use.

In one important respect, there was an absolute dearth in the British Isles. The sailing ship depended for her mobility on the strength of her masts. These could be constructed from composite pieces – 'made masts' – but the process was complex and the result not always satisfactory. The ideal single-tree mast required not only strength but suppleness. Its usefulness depended on the continued presence of resin in the trunk. Scots pine was found to be too coarse and the best wood for the purpose, at least until the resources of New Hampshire and Maine could be developed more fully, was that of the *Pinus silvestris* from the Baltic region. England's need was also Holland's.

The Dutch supplied herrings, salt from Biscay, wine from France and the Mediterranean to the northern countries. In return, and largely from Danzig and Riga, they loaded corn and timber (and refined wood products such as ash), as well as pitch, tar, flax and hemp. From Sweden they drew copper and iron. Without such supplies their flourishing shipyards would soon have been idle. When conditions allowed, Dutch ships were engaged,

49

alongside English vessels, in carrying such essential naval stores to English dockyards.

Trouble in the north was dynastic. Denmark had long controlled Norway, and it had been a Danish aspiration that the Scandinavian kingdoms might coalesce. They did so for a time, after the Union of Kalmar of 1397, under the leadership of the Danish Queen, Margaret. The Union did not survive, even as a formal arrangement, and there was no hope of retaining Sweden when Gustavus Vasa won power in 1523.

It so happened that during the seventeenth century two exceptional men reigned contemporaneously in Denmark and Sweden. The Danish sovereign, Christian IV, had outstanding vitality, versatility and distinction, and was the only king ever to have lost an eye in a naval engagement. Unfortunately, his timing was poor. His intervention in continental affairs during the course of the Thirty Years' War between Catholic and Protestant states was as unhappy for Denmark as that of Gustavus Adolphus was brilliant.

Gustavus Adolphus and his troops, the famed 'Blue Boys', became the spearhead of the Protestant cause until the king's death at Lützen in 1632. By that time he had made his country's voice powerful in Europe. He was succeeded by his young daughter, Christina, who grew into an eccentric. Her reign could have ended disastrously had she not, after much heart-searching, decided to become a Roman Catholic and to abdicate in favour of her German cousin, who succeeded her as Charles X Adolphus.

Just as alliance with the Danes had helped the Dutch during the course of the war with England, preventing valuable supplies from reaching English ports, so Cromwell looked hopefully to Sweden, all the more so since she was a leading Protestant power. He sent the highly intelligent Bulstrode Whitelock on a mission to Stockholm. This led to an interesting account of the court of Queen Christina, but to no firm alliance. Whitelock discovered that Swedish merchants were exempt from Sound dues, and were much concerned about English incursions into the Baltic. The Protector was slowly discovering what acute observers could have told him years earlier – that the motives behind national policy were changing. Religion, the cause of so much bloodshed, was yielding to other considerations, although it was still to account for terrible mischief and persecution. The Dutch were primarily interested in making money. The Swedish king, to whom religion meant little – he was a hard-headed hard-drinking soldier of fantastic energy – was bent on enlarging the inheritance of Gustavus Adolphus into an empire controlled by himself.

Charles X, whose exploits are commemorated in the Palace of Drottningholm in a series of paintings and a vast wall-map recording his astonishing marches, directed his energies first against Poland. His excuse was that the King, John Casimir, laid claim to the throne of Sweden. Much of Charles's revenue came from customs he levied at river mouths in his possession, and it was natural that he should wish to add to them that of the Vistula. He won victories against incredible odds, and was so advanced in warlike technique that a primitive machine-gun is among the relics of his reign. But he was unable to hold his conquests through lack of manpower for garrisons, a predicament which became acute when roving Russian armies appeared against him.

The Swedish position improved when Charles entered into a series of agreements with the Elector of Brandenburg. Even so, his siege and blockade of Danzig ended in failure during the summer of 1656, for at this point the Dutch, their corn cargoes interrupted, had to intervene. They had no wish to be embroiled in a war with Sweden, but the presence of the aristocratic Admiral Jacob van Wassenaer, Lord of Obdam, together with de Ruyter, de With, Cornelius Tromp and a powerful fleet, made Charles realise that his aim was hopeless. The fact was emphasised by a brief appearance off the Polish port of a Danish squadron sent by Frederick III.

The situation changed during the following year. Frederick III decided to attack Sweden in the hope of regaining territory lost in earlier wars, and the Emperor Leopold sent troops to aid Catholic Poland. Charles reacted vigorously. Recognising Denmark as the weaker of his enemies, he invaded Jutland, which he overran. He next contemplated an assault on Copenhagen, but his successes were neutralised by the defection of Brandenburg. The elector's support for Poland was bought, in defiance of obligations to Sweden, with the grant of sovereignty over East Prussia.

At this stage Charles appealed to Cromwell for money and ships, and was told that the price of help would be the cession of Bremen, then in Swedish hands, since the Protector considered the port a convenient means of access to the Protestant states of North Germany. Charles found the stipulation too stiff, and the only English help was diplomatic.

Cromwell had tried to project Charles as a Protestant crusader, but few were deceived. The king's immediate aim was to turn the Baltic into a Swedish lake, and to do this he must overcome Denmark. The task proved easy. Frederick III was no military genius; his nobles were unreliable, and his army was inferior to that of the

Admiral Obdam, commanding the
Dutch at the Battle of the Sound
print after Honthorst   Prinz
Hendrick Museum, Rotterdam

Swedes. Charles was able by force of arms and astounding marches across the frozen Belt to threaten Copenhagen and to dictate a treaty at Roskilde, burial place of Danish kings, in February 1658. It was the highest point in his career. Frederick ceded the provinces of Scania, Halland, and other territory and islands. Even this humiliation was not enough. Charles soon found a pretext to renew the war. He captured and slighted the magnificent castle of Kronborg at Elsinore, the pride of Christian IV and a fitting background for Shakespeare's *Hamlet*. By the end of the summer his armies, using artillery taken from Kronborg, invested Copenhagen. It is probable that the Danish capital would have fallen, despite a stout resistance by the citizens, had not Holland and England decided to intervene. Both countries were by this time justifiably alarmed at the intention of Charles to control both sides of the Sound, and thereby to admit or exclude the passage of foreign ships at will. The alternative route to the Baltic, by way of Great and Little Belts, presented navigational difficulties, and in any case could be blocked by whoever controlled the long-established fortifications on either side of the entrances.

Cromwell's illness and death in September 1658 gave the Dutch the chance to act first, and a fleet was sent to the Baltic under Obdam, now Lieutenant-Admiral of Holland. The Dutch representative in Denmark, van Beuningen, had urged Frederick to rely on the long-standing alliance and to disregard the terms of Roskilde. He told the king that 'the oaken keys of the Sound lie in the docks of Amsterdam'. When the moment of crisis came, his words were justified. Obdam anchored outside the Sound on 23 October. The Swedes were then off Elsinore, their fleet in charge of Admiral Karl Wrangel. The Swedes had superior numbers, but as Obdam had as his Vice-Admirals de With and Floriszoon, both with much war experience, and reliable captains, he could regard the prospect before him with reasonable confidence.

The fleets got under way about the same time in the early morning of 29 October. Obdam ran the gauntlet of the batteries mounted at Kronborg unharmed, in spite of heavy fire. The Dutch advanced without much order, and since there was a strong wind from a northerly direction, a *mêlée* was the natural result. Flying his flag in the *Brederode*, de With attacked the Swedish commander-in-chief in the *Viktoria*, but on the appearance of Obdam in the *Eendracht* he relinquished the place of honour and set about the smaller ships *Drake* and *Leopard*. The *Leopard* he drove off so badly damaged that she was put ashore on the island of Hven and burnt, but soon afterwards the *Drake* and

The Dutch ship *Eendracht*, flagship of
Obdam, off Kronborg Castle during
the campaign of 1658   *Herman
Witmont*   NMMG

the *Brederode* went ashore together on the Danish side of the
channel. The *Drake* got off, but the *Brederode* remained fast, and
was fiercely attacked by the *Wismar*. After two hours raking fire
the Swedes boarded, de With was killed and his flagship taken.
Almost immediately afterwards she slipped into deeper water and
sank, depriving the victors of a notable prize.

Meanwhile, the *Drake* had gone to the relief of Wrangel in the
Viktoria, which was hard-pressed by Obdam and his captains. The
Swedish flagship was in fact so much damaged that when at last
she shook off her opponents, Wrangel had to take her out of
action and anchor for repairs.

Obdam in his turn was being battered, particularly by the
Caesar, which earlier in the day had attacked the *Joshua* and killed
Vice-Admiral Floriszoon in the process, but the Dutch com-
mander-in-chief was well supported by his captains and got clear.

Four Swedish ships lowered their colours during the course of
the morning. The Dutch *Breda* was also lost, but the enemy
abandoned her when a fire broke out aboard and allowed Obdam
to recover her later. Intermittent fighting continued until the early
afternoon, when the wind freshened, and Obdam signalled his
fleet to reassemble for the run towards Copenhagen. Even if they
had been disposed so to do, few Swedish ships were in any state
to follow. Although Wrangel and Charles were to claim a

victory on the score that the Dutch left the area of conflict first, there was little justification for this view. Obdam's purpose had been from the outset to reach Copenhagen, reinforce the Dutch squadron in the harbour, break the Swedish blockade, and raise the landward siege.

On the Dutch side, the only capital loss was the *Brederode*, famous as having been at one time Tromp's flagship. Of the four large Swedish ships captured, one sank later. But in sum the Dutch paid a high price for helping their friends in the death of two such eminent flag officers as de With and Floriszoon.

During the evening of the day of battle, six Danish ships joined Obdam off Hven. The allies then proceeded to Copenhagen, where Obdam received acclamation from the Danes. Frederick III was a connoisseur and bibliophile, and the Dutch lieutenant-admiral took pleasure in showing him a record made during the course of the action from a light craft by Willem van der Velde. He and his equally accomplished son were forerunners of the official war artists who were to record so many later sea campaigns. The pair had an artistic career which extended from before the Anglo-Dutch war of Cromwell's time to the earlier years of the eighteenth century. 'I have shown Their Majesties the sketch of the Battle by Mr. van de Velde of Amsterdam,' wrote Obdam proudly, 'and it has pleased Their Majesties exceedingly.'

Despite the reverse inflicted on him by the Dutch, Charles X was not prepared to soften his attitude towards the Danes or to moderate his long-term ambitions. His prevailing mood was anger at Obdam's interference, and once again he looked to England as a counterweight to Dutch and Danish predominance. Sir George Ayscue went to Sweden with a squadron of twenty-one ships, and was accorded admiral's rank in the Swedish service. His force could be of no immediate use, however, for it did not sail until the beginning of November and did not reach the Sound until the onset of severe winter weather made a return journey necessary, Ayscue staying in Sweden. It was realised in London, where word was not received of Obdam's fight until after Ayscue had sailed, that if Charles were to be badly worsted, a Dutch–Danish combination could close the Baltic to foreign shipping as effectually as a Swedish victory.

Being alarmed at the continuing state of Baltic affairs, Admiral Mountagu was sent to the Sound in charge of a fleet of some sixty ships in the following spring. His strength was enough to give

Dutch and Swedish ships engaged at
the Battle of the Sound   *Willem
de Velde the Elder*   NMMG

pause before any ill-considered move was made by Dutch or
Danes. The diplomats were also busy, and in May 1659 England,
France and the United Provinces agreed to a convention, signed at
the Hague, that the signatory powers should jointly mediate to
try to bring about a settlement based on the Treaty of Roskilde.
This was followed by two further agreements between England
and the United Provinces to deal with the uncompromising attitude of Charles X. The maritime powers undertook to use their
fleets to compel Sweden and Denmark to accept terms rather less
favourable to Sweden than the Treaty of Roskilde.

As has so often been the case, the mediators found that neither
party desired peace on any such basis as was proposed. Denmark
was unwilling to treat alone, wishing to consult Brandenburg,
whose elector was the most formidable of Charles's enemies
ashore. Charles, for his part, regarded any delay in campaigning
as being unfavourable to his prospects. He was indignant to find
that the English, supposedly his friends, and the Dutch, his known
foes, had already agreed on the terms of a settlement they thought
to be fit and proper. He insisted that he wanted mediators, not
judges, and warned the representatives of the maritime powers that
if their proposals were based on fleets, his projects were based on

armies. When matters were drifting into an impasse, Mountagu's sudden decision to take his fleet back to England reduced her influence accordingly, and she took no important part in future negotiations.

The Dutch *Brederode*, once Tromp's flagship, and sunk later at the Battle of the Sound   *Willem van de Velde the Younger*   NMMG

Mountagu's decision arose from the fact that he realised there was likely to be a strong movement afoot in England to restore the Stuarts. He wished to be on hand to ensure that events should run as much as possible in his own favour. His motives might have been more lofty but when in the following year Charles II 'came into his own again', as the saying was, Mountagu's influence in the fleet was as great as Monck's in the army, and both men, able servants of Parliament as they had been, played prominent parts in ensuring that the Restoration was peaceful. In February 1660, shortly before that event took place, Charles X died most unexpectedly, with current Baltic problems unsolved.

de Ruyter had replaced Obdam as senior Dutch officer in Baltic waters, and had received orders from home to assume a vigorous offensive. As soon as news of Charles's death reached Holland, policy altered and the admiral was instructed to take no further part in hostilities. Being de Ruyter, he used his own discretion. When the Swedes appeared intent on renewing a blockade of

Copenhagen he told their commander that such action would bring about an attack. Sperling, the officer concerned, took the hint and withdrew to Landscrona.

A peace treaty was signed in the Danish capital on 27 May 1660. As had been expected, it restored to Denmark some of the territory Charles had gained at Roskilde. The question of the prevention of foreign shipping from entering the Baltic was dropped. de Ruyter returned to Holland three months later.

The Battle of the Sound did not by any means signify an end to the struggle for control of the Baltic. It was a proof that no nation with extensive maritime interests and a strong navy would be likely to allow·control to pass wholly either to Denmark or Sweden. Such nations were also likely to fight to ensure the freedom of ships from foreign countries to go about their business unmolested in northern waters. England, France and Holland were all later to send fleets into the Baltic at times of crisis for the same purpose as the States-General had sent Obdam, for the north continued to be a constant scene of war and traffic was at times interrupted. Sweden gradually lost the empire acquired by Gustavus Adolphus and Charles X. The Danish kings, much reduced in power, continued to exact Sound dues at Elsinore. The dues had become an anachronism by 1857, and they were commuted for the sum of £4 million, subscribed by the principal maritime nations.

4 Anson and the Spanish Treasure

If combined efforts did much to thwart national ambitions to achieve absolute supremacy in the Baltic in the seventeenth century, the notion of a monopoly of power in any given maritime area remained a factor in international affairs. This was particularly true so far as Spain was concerned, after the discoveries of Columbus and other oceanic pioneers.

As early as 1494, at the Treaty of Tordesillas, Pope Alexander VI, in a way which was at once arbitrary and commanding, divided the world into two great sectors of influence. Portugal was made paramount in Africa, and to the east of that continent; Spain was given dominance in a westerly direction, although the demarcation allowed Brazil to Portugal. This partitioned the world in a way which altogether froze out three future maritime powers – France, England and Holland – which had had no part in the negotiations.

Spain rejoiced in such a mandate. After Philip II had annexed Portugal in 1580, he could fairly regard the world beyond Europe as his oyster. It is true that François I of France remarked, 'I should very much like to see the clause in Adam's will that excludes me from a share of the world', and that Elizabeth of England's privateers, and those from Holland, blithely disregarded the papal edict.

Even so, and especially in the Pacific, the fact was that a Spanish monopoly held good for generations. It was not seriously disputed by England between the time of Drake's circumnavigation and George Anson's equally memorable feat, achieved between 1740 and 1744. Anson's venture brought him wealth 'beyond the dreams of avarice', and an influence on his country's naval affairs even greater than Drake's had been in an earlier era.

Anson, an officer of forty-three who had already seen much service, was picked for an independent naval command in a war which had broken out with Spain the year before he sailed. Another, and far more important foray, which was to be led by Admiral Edward Vernon, was aimed at enemy possessions in the

Caribbean, since the cause of conflict, nominally at any rate, was Spanish interference with British trade in the West Indies and on the Spanish Main. Actually, the country was in a warlike temper. It was popularly believed that the Spanish colonial empire was ripe for plucking, and a potential source for an enormous export traffic. The view of Spanish decadence had something to support it, though in general it was premature. The war itself was to develop into a complex dynastic struggle typical of its era, in which many countries became involved.

The expedition was the most disgracefully manned ever to have set out. If the Board of Admiralty responsible for the arrangements had been lined up and shot, it would have been no more than just. To make matters worse, security was so bad that the Spaniards knew all about the expedition before ever it set sail. The plain fact was that Vernon, being senior to Anson and in charge of a

more important operation, had first pick of everything.

Anson's squadron consisted of the *Centurion*, 60 guns, 8 years old; the *Gloucester*, 50 guns, 3 years old; the *Severn*, 48 guns, dating back to 1695, though since rebuilt; the *Pearl*, 42 guns, 30 years old; the *Wager*, 24 guns, which had been bought for the navy in 1739; and the *Tryal*, a sloop of 14 guns, 8 years old. Two supply ships accompanied the men-of-war, the *Anna* and the *Industry*.

At least half the seamen were press-ganged. Among the cream of the rest were 39 volunteers from Jersey, who were obtained through the medium of Lieutenant Saumarez of the *Centurion*, himself a Channel Islander. As soldiers were thought to be necessary to form landing-parties to storm Spanish positions ashore, 259 outpatients from Chelsea Hospital were conscripted. Almost all of them were 60 years of age, and some over 70. Several had

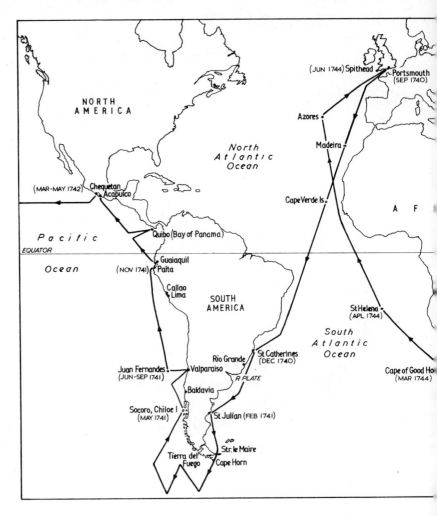

lost limbs. Most of them were too infirm to desert before sailing, but those who could chose to risk the death penalty rather than face life aboard a man-of-war. 'Indeed,' wrote Anson in his account, 'it is difficult to conceive a more moving scene than the embarkation of these unhappy veterans.' Of the ancients who set out, not one survived. The rest of the marine regiment was made up of 210 raw recruits, some of whom had never handled a musket.

The voyage began on 18 September 1740, Anson's orders being to prey on Spanish shipping in the Pacific, or the South Seas as the area was then called. He was also to attack towns and settlements on the coasts of Chile and Peru – the Indians of the Spanish colonial empire, grossly exploited as they were, being considered ripe for rebellion. These ideas were suggested by officials of the bankrupt South Seas Company, which had never sent a single

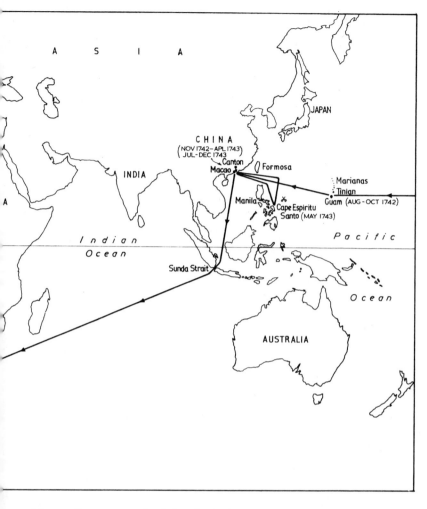

ship to the area, and of the flourishing East India Company who wished for a show of force in the hope of aiding trade.

Drake's exploits in Elizabeth's time were well-remembered, and public imagination had been stimulated by William Dampier's *Voyage Round the World*, issued in 1697 and widely read. Later, a highly successful Bristol privateer, Woodes Rogers, had in the earlier years of the eighteenth century roved in the South Seas. He had rescued Alexander Selkirk, the original of Robinson Crusoe, from the island of Juan Fernandez, where he had been marooned. Woodes Rogers had also written a book, *A Cruizing Voyage Round the World*, which appeared in 1712. He had gathered much treasure which he tried to increase by leasing the Bahamas, only to find himself in danger from pirates as treasure-minded as himself.

The great prize of such a voyage as Anson's might not be from raiding, but the capture of one of the treasure galleons which made the 8,000 mile voyage between Acapulco in Mexico and Manila in the Philippines. Westbound, the ship would be loaded with coin and bullion for trade with the orient; eastbound, her cargo would consist of silk, spices, porcelain, and the various luxuries enjoyed by Europeans, to whom the goods would be re-exported. With determination, accurate timing, and skill at arms, such a capture was not beyond the bounds of possibility.

The delays due to manning difficulties, and the order to escort an outward-bound convoy during the initial stages of his voyage, robbed Anson of any chance of surprise. Even the usually dilatory Spaniards organised an intercepting force of five powerful ships under Don José Pizarro, which sailed from Santander in October. In the upshot, Pizarro met the same dreadful weather in the south Atlantic as Anson, and all but one of his ships were wrecked. Anson's main enemies were disease, incessant storms, lack of adequate charts, and inability to find longitude with any degree of accuracy in days before reliable time-keepers were available at sea. He reached the latitude of Cape Horn at a time of year when the westerlies were at their fiercest, and they spared him nothing.

By the time the Pacific-island haven of Juan Fernandez was reached, the squadron was reduced to the *Centurion*, the *Gloucester* and the *Tryal* sloop. They had already lost two-thirds of their people, the survivors being so spent that they could scarcely work the ships. The *Wager* had been wrecked, carrying with her all the artillery necessary for successful land operations. Anson's one stroke of luck was that a second Spanish force of interception ordered to Juan Fernandez left shortly before his arrival, believing that Cape Horn storms had defeated the commodore, like many before him. Enfeebled by battered ships, they would have been an easy prey – and the Spaniards had instructions to spare no one.

It was weeks before Anson at last felt his men to be refreshed enough to resume their mission: he had no thought of turning back. His resources were so reduced that he could now only hope to take such prizes as he could outsail and out-gun. This he duly did, acquiring some treasure in the process, and amazing the Spaniards by his humane courtesy towards his prisoners. He also sacked Paita, on the coast of Peru, with unexpected ease. He then headed north for Acapulco, on the chance of surprising the Manila galleon. Here, luck was against him; the Spaniards had been warned, and the place itself was far too strong for Anson to attack with the forlorn remnant of his marine regiment.

By this stage the *Gloucester* was in such bad shape that only a long spell in dockyard hands could have saved her. The crew were worn out with working at the pumps, so she was scuttled. Though still seaworthy the gallant little *Tryal*, which had survived the Horn, was also destroyed so that her officers and men could serve in the flagship. Scurvy – the disease due to lack of vitamin C – once again took hold. Yet Anson was now faced with a long westward run over vast stretches of ocean to the coast of China. When he put in to refresh at the Ladrones, he narrowly missed catastrophe. His now triply precious flagship was driven by stress of weather from her anchorage. She was so delayed in making a hazardous return that Anson, with his usual imperturbability, set about making a boat from the resources of Tinian. This was designed to be large enough to hold all those with him.

The *Centurion* rejoined and Anson duly set out for Macao, where he arrived in November 1742. He now had a total effective force of only 210 officers and men out of the 1,500 or so which had made up his original strength. He had little to show, in comparison with what he had lost in men and ships. His difficulties were increased rather than diminished by the attitude of the Chinese who, to all intents and purposes, controlled the concession despite a Portuguese presence. As he was in charge of a regular man-of-war, Anson refused to pay port dues, which would have established an unfortunate precedent. The local mandarins thereupon refused him essential supplies, and he found himself unwelcome even to the captains of East Indiamen whose trade depended on a precarious balance of interests, on acts of face-saving, on bribery, and on custom.

Patience won. By April 1743, after five months, Anson considered that the *Centurion* had been satisfactorily refitted and supplied, although she had not much more than half her normal complement of 400. Officially, she left Macao homeward bound via Batavia. Actually, Anson had a shrewd idea that with patience and skill he could intercept a Manila galleon as she approached Cape Espiritu Santo. This promontory, on the Philippine island of Samar, was the Spaniard's usual landfall preliminary to the difficult inshore course to the chief Philippine port and capital.

Anson's own security was better than that of the home authorities before his expedition sailed. Nevertheless, there were suspicions of his design both at Manila and elsewhere. Preparations had been made to provide an escort and protection for the galleon as she approached Samar, but these were lackadaisical and never amounted to any real threat to the *Centurion*.

A few days out from Macao the commodore called his men together and told them his idea. The effect was immediate; zeal and excitement attended every future sighting. Although so reduced, the ship's company was made up of those who had already survived misfortunes which had proved too much for most of their companions. They had been reinforced by 23 Lascars and a few Dutchmen locally recruited, making a total of 227 men and boys at quarters. With a stout ship, plenty of ammunition, and the prospect of prize-money, all responded to the intensive training in gunnery and musketry which Anson proceeded to conduct (well beyond sight of land, and at first to the north of the Philippines). There were not enough gunners for regular broadsides, so Anson organised mobile teams to serve the guns successively. A character called Jacob Blackbeard became leader of the marksmen stationed in the fighting tops, ready to pick off Spaniards on the galleon's upper deck.

Cruising lasted from 19 April until 20 June. Then, at sunrise, the quarry came in sight and on exactly the course anticipated. In his narrative, Anson was to call her the *Nostra Signora de Cabadonga*; other accounts refer to her with slight differences – as they do many of the islands, including Samar which Anson knew as Samal.

Propaganda being as old as history, it is noteworthy that common talk was to refer to the duel between the *Centurion* and the *Cabadonga* as being like that of David and Goliath. Even contemporary marine painters, their work based on sketches and details supplied by combatants to such accomplished artists as Samuel Scott, do not give the lie to this interpretation. Recent research, notably by Dr Glyndwr Williams, has shown how false it is.

The *Centurion* had been designed and built as a ship of war, and her men had been trained to a hair. She carried 60 guns, 24 of them 24-pounders. She had muskets available for all who were likely to be able to use them. She was about 20ft longer on her gun deck than the *Cabadonga*, and was of just over 1,000 tons burden, whereas that of the Spaniard was about 700 tons.

The *Cabadonga* was freighted low in the water and had no lower tier of gunports. As ordnance she carried nothing heavier than 12-pounders, and although the numbers on board – 530 all told – were much in excess of what was carried by the English ship (a fact on which the Spanish captain relied), a high proportion were militarily valueless. They were passengers, servants, convicts and so on, untrained in war, and in action a mere impediment. Only 266 were members of the crew. Half were Filipinos.

The *Cabadonga*'s Commander, Don Gerónimo Montero, was an unwise man. He had been warned of the possibility that Anson might be in wait for him, yet he took no serious pre-

Anson's capture of the Manila galleon, 1743   *Samuel Scott*
NMMG

cautions – not because he disbelieved the threat existed, but out of ineffable confidence in his ship, her guns, and his crew. He **was** guilty of what students of war know as 'picture-making', that is creating an image of an enemy in the guise in which it is desired to meet him. He pictured Anson's men as half-starved and in-efficient, as well as few in numbers. Anson's First-Lieutenant, Philip Saumarez, wrote the apt comment on such a notion: 'We were amazed to think what he could propose against our weight of metal and a ship of our appearance.'

The action began a little after midday and lasted less than two hours. The Spaniards made no attempt to run, but stood up boldly to the attack and even made preparations to board. Jacob Blackbeard's top-men, thirty in all, first drove the enemy from their own fighting tops and then, in Anson's account, 'made prodigious havoc with their small-arms, killing or wounding every officer but one that ever appeared on the quarter-deck, and wounding in particular the General of the galleon himself'. Montero, a Portuguese by birth, was struck in the chest. He gave orders from the cock-pit to blow up the ship, but he was dis-regarded and the colours were struck. Anson had one sailor killed, another died of wounds, a third died after an amputation, and there were sixteen wounded, including a lieutenant. When Saumarez was sent across to take charge of the prize, he stated that the galleon's decks 'afforded such a scene as may be supposed after a sharp dispute, being promiscuously covered with carcasses, entrails and dismembered limbs'.

The *Cabadonga* was taken and the voyage 'made' in the sense that Anson had won the richest prize recorded, but his difficulties were not over. He had 492 prisoners, 170 of whom were wounded; the *Centurion* had not emerged scot-free, and the *Cabadonga* was in a precarious state. The treasure had to be transferred, and Anson had then to return to the Canton river for supplies and to land the Spaniards. He could expect no joyous welcome from the mandarins, who had been only too glad to see him depart. He would need all his diplomacy, and a certain amount of luck, to get his treasure back to England. Even the weather turned uncertain, with sudden squalls and showers of rain, and he had no reliable charts to cover an area of sea which he knew to be full of hazards.

The treasure was prodigious. More and more was discovered in the recesses of the *Cabadonga*, including bullion concealed in what appeared to be cheeses. There were 1,313,843 'pieces of eight', a coin of the value of eight reales and equivalent to a peso, or Spanish dollar. In addition there were 35,682 ounces of virgin silver. Well could Anson have echoed the words of the Queen of Sheba after visiting Solomon – 'behold, the half was not told me' – and the more the galleon was ransacked the more the wonder grew.

The first serious alarm was from a French ship. Anson, without recent news from home, was uncertain whether war with France had succeeded war with Spain, which was not an un-common pattern. Fortunately, the Frenchman, who was equally ill-informed, made off, and when the respective commanders encountered one another later near Canton, they decided on discretion. Even so, the Frenchman did some harm to Anson in that he was able to persuade the mandarins to put all the obstacles they could in the way of Anson's obtaining supplies. The officials needed little urging to pursue a course so natural to them.

The *Centurion* and her prize anchored at Macao on 11 July 1743 and then moved forty miles up the river. Once again Anson refused to pay port dues and this naturally made things no easier with the mandarins, one of whose perplexities was why the commodore, who they considered to be the Great Ladrone or pirate, did not chop off the heads of his prisoners. On this visit, Anson managed to persuade the supercargoes of the East India Company's ships not to trade with the Chinese until his wants were met. This gave him valuable bargaining power and, incidentally, raised the prestige of the company.

Patience had rewarded Anson on his first visit to China. On his second, being in a stronger position, he decided, after a decent interval, to take matters into his own hands. Having waited three months for the necessary permission from the viceroy to purchase all necessary stores, Anson decided to attend the potentate in person and in state. Inviting the principal East India Company servants to accompany him, he organised a retinue of forty seamen dressed in brilliantly coloured uniforms of scarlet and blue with silver buckles on their shoes, and wearing large tricornes. A stately progress was made by barge, with the usual musical accompaniment, to the main city of Canton where the party was given accommodation in the premises of the East India Company.

At that time, Canton had a million inhabitants. It was looked upon by Europeans as a source of wonder and enlightenment. Inside the Great Wall was the viceroy's sumptuous residence, or Yamen. This was set in a green park amid flowering jasmine trees, with deer roaming everywhere. Along the river bank were warehouses belonging to English, Dutch, French, Swedish and Danish traders. Amid such splendour, Anson waited. One excuse after another was offered for the viceroy's inability to meet him.

At last, luck altered the course of events for the better. A serious fire broke out, the Chinese seemed incapable of coping with it, and a party of seamen from the *Centurion* were the means by which the larger part of the city was saved. This impressed the mandarins so much that within a single day a message came through that the viceroy was ready to receive the commodore.

The meeting was on a regal scale. Anson was borne to the palace in a canopied chair, hung with gold and silver brocade, by sixteen uniformed coolies. He was attended by Saumarez, Lieutenant Keppel, aged seventeen, the captains of the East Indiamen, and the forty sailors who, in their gaudy attire, had rowed the party to the city. Alone of the Europeans, Anson was permitted to sit down. This was to be a meeting of dignitaries of equal rank.

The viceroy was genuinely curious. It was his first acquaintance with a European, and he was interested in the fact that Anson had come not to trade, but merely to provision. He did not kill his enemies, which was odd, but treated them more like friends.

Finally, this strange creature would not obey the rules by paying harbour dues, and was ready to reinforce his decision with a broadside. The viceroy, having listened to Anson through an intelligent interpreter, showed understanding. Anson's requests were granted, and no further mention was made of harbour dues. In this way, neither party lost face.

Once supplies were aboard, the last piece of business was to dispose of the *Cabadonga* which was in an even poorer condition than when she had arrived, for there had been little opportunity to refit her. It was made known to Anson that the Spaniards would be glad of her return, whatever her condition. A Portuguese syndicate was instructed to be responsible for the prisoners, and to offer the sum of $6,000 for the hull. This was accepted. Anson was at last free to sail for old England. In December, he left the Canton river.

The journey home, by way of the Cape of Good Hope, was uneventful except for one last escape. On 10 June 1744, after a six-month passage, Anson entered the Channel. There he was told by the captain of a privateer that there had been war with France since the previous March. Anson's own words are surely the best conclusion to his adventures.

> . . . that the signal perils which had so often threatened them in the preceding part of the enterprize, might pursue them to the very last, Mr. Anson learnt on his arrival that there was a French fleet of considerable force cruising in the chops of the Channel, which, by the account of their position, he found the *Centurion* had run through, and been all the time concealed by a fog. Thus was this expedition finished, when it had lasted three years and nine months, after having, by its event, evinced this important truth. That though prudence, intrepidity, and perseverance united are not exempted from the blows of adverse fortune; yet in a long series of transactions, they usually rise superior to its power, and in the end rarely fail of proving successful.

The commodore anchored off the Isle of Wight on 15 June. Soon there began a triumphant procession of thirty-two packed wagon-loads of treasure, which took the road from Portsmouth to the Tower of London. Vernon had failed on the Spanish Main. How differently Anson had fared in the Pacific!

Henceforward, he was always at or near the centre of events. The year after the completion of his voyage he got his flag; then he beat the French in battle off Cape Finisterre. A peerage followed, and marriage to Lord Chancellor Hardwicke's daughter. He had two spells as 1st Lord of the Admiralty, during which he reorganised the navy. He died in 1762.

His lasting memorials are diverse. In 1748 *A Voyage Round the World* appeared, 'Compiled from Papers and other Materials of the Right Honourable George, Lord Anson, and published under his Direction by Richard Walter, M.A., Chaplain of his Majesty's Ship the *Centurion* . . .'. The book included a fulsome dedication to the Duke of Bedford by Richard Walter, formerly a Fellow of Sidney Sussex College, Cambridge, from which it could be inferred that he drafted the text, although he himself went home from China before the capture of the galleon. Actually, the chief writer was known to contemporaries such as Lieutenant-Colonel Cracherode, the senior officer of the marine regiment, to have been Benjamin Robins. He was an able pamphleteer and, incidentally, the foremost ballistics expert in Europe. This fact was later overlooked, and what seems to have happened was that Robins drafted the bulk of the text, Walter read the proofs, and Anson, naturally, supervised the whole. The work, which in its own day was a best-seller, has been favourite reading ever since.

So cruel had been the sufferings of the squadron from scurvy, particularly during the earlier part of the voyage, that this inspired James Lind, a Scots naval surgeon, to conduct a controlled dietetic experiment in HMS *Salisbury*, the results of which were published in 1753. The salient fact revealed was that orange- or lemon-juice were sovereign remedies (lemon-juice being twice as efficacious as lime). Much the same facts had been discovered by individual captains in earlier times, but they had not been publicised and were thus forgotten. It took the navy over forty years to accept Lind's proof, by which time he was dead. Even afterwards matters were mishandled, for in the 1860s lime-juice was substituted for lemon because it was cheaper. It was an indifferent choice, and there is at least some excuse, historically, for the contemptuous undertone in the use of the word 'limey' for an Englishman.

The *Centurion* survived until 1769, and added to her honours. She was at the battle of Finisterre in Anson's fleet, at the capture of Louisbourg during the Seven Years' War, and in Saunders's fleet which carried the assault up the St Lawrence to Quebec in the 'Year of Victories', 1759. She was at Havana the year Anson died. The country owed much to her qualities, and she was not broken up until 1769.

Anson was a Staffordshire man. He was born at Shugborough where, after his voyage, he rebuilt the family home on behalf of

Chinese house at Shugborough, Staffordshire, designed by one of Anson's captains　National Trust

his elder brother Thomas. It was on a grander scale and 'at the expense of his country's enemies', as the phrase was. Thomas Anson was a man of taste, and on his recommendation James ('Athenian') Stuart was employed to embellish the grounds. Lord and Lady Anson had no children, and Thomas Anson became heir to the fortune. Out of this, he commissioned Stuart to build him a house which still stands in St James's Square. Shugborough, as a property of the National Trust, contains many reminders of the circumnavigation. Not the least enchanting is the Chinese House designed in 1747 by Peircy Brett, one of Anson's ablest officers.

Although all ended so well for Anson, the voyage left a trail of bitterness among certain others. For in the course of a long legal battle, only the *Centurion's* regular complement were accorded their regulation share of prize-money. The rest, whatever their naval rank, had only a seaman's share, as being 'supernumerary to the establishment' – this in spite of the fact that they had taken their appropriate part in the action with the *Cabadonga*. Precedent won; friendships proved in storm and battle were broken. Even so, merely to have completed that astonishing voyage was an achievement from which nothing could detract.

5 The British Take Manila

Anson was in charge at the admiralty for almost the entire span of the Seven Years' War with France, and later with Spain (1756–62). It was marked by success for British arms, and the expansion of an empire which has dissolved only during our own time. The chief War Minister, William Pitt, favoured combined operations in which navy and army, after a slow start, gradually learnt co-operation. After a failure before Rochefort and a very limited success at St Malo, there came a succession of victories – Louisbourg in 1758, Quebec the year after, and Havana three years later still. The last such triumph, one which would have been specifically gratifying to Anson had he lived to receive news of it, was the capture of Manila. This event took place within a few weeks of the admiral's death, but he had attended the meeting of ministers who considered the plan which was entrusted to the navy jointly with the East India Company.

Anson was well-placed to understand the problems involved in such an operation and the reasons which might justify it, through his experiences in the expedition of twenty years before. It was suggested that the Spaniards, now that they had entered the war, might interfere with British facilities at Canton if not prevented. There was also the hope that Manila might serve as an *entrepôt* for additional trade. Its capture would certainly afford a bargaining-point in any settlement; indeed, the orders from the government envisaged a colony at Mindanao, the most southerly of the larger Philippine islands, 'which could be kept after the peace'. Finally, there was the prospect of loot by land and sea.

The Philippines, whose inhabitants derived chiefly from Malayan or Chinese stock, had been discovered in 1521 on the voyage of the Portuguese navigator Magellan during the course of the first European circumnavigation. Manila, the capital, had been founded half a century later by the *conquistador* Legaspi, who subdued the inhabitants of many of the islands. Friars are alleged to have converted them to Christianity. The Spaniards, however, for all the extent of the trade which passed through Manila, had a

very loose hold on the people and took no great interest in
defence. In spite of Anson's capture of the galleon in 1743, the
garrison had no fear of intruders and considered Manila safe so
long as relations with China were peaceful.

Although in background and character the chief executants
appointed to the Manila operation could scarcely have been more
in contrast, they made an efficient team. The sea officer in overall
charge was Rear-Admiral Samuel Cornish. He had seen hard
service, and had risen to flag rank without the advantage of gentle
birth or formal education. He had arrived in India in 1759, and
succeeded to the command of a force of third- and fourth-rate
ships of the line on the death of Admiral Charles Steevens. He also
inherited from his predecessor a flag captain of outstanding ability.
This was Richard Kempenfelt. His forbears were from the nobility
of Sweden, and the captain was the son of an equally admirable
soldier. He figures in the pages which Steele and Addison wrote
for *The Spectator* as 'Captain Sentry', who is described as 'a
Gentleman of great Courage, good Understanding, but invincible
Modesty': like father, like son. Kempenfelt had served in operations in the Far East under a succession of chiefs, all of whom sang
his praises. He was also well known to Colonel William Draper,
who was to be Admiral Cornish's opposite number, being in
charge of the troops.

Draper had been at Eton and King's College, Cambridge, and
was a classical scholar. A man of means, he had elected to serve in
the Guards and had later raised a regiment of his own, the 79th of
Foot, which he commanded at the siege of the French at Fort St
George. Draper, who had spent some time at Canton on sick-leave
from India, forwarded a detailed plan for an assault on Manila to
the home authorities. This was adopted. Draper himself was given
the local rank of brigadier-general, and was told that although no
troops could be sent out to him from England he was to use what
could be spared from the garrisons of the sub-continent.

The brains of Draper and Kempenfelt and the unexpected spur
of obstruction from the East India Company had a stimulating
effect on the two armed services, for they worked in harmony
throughout. The attitude of the company arose from the fact that
a vessel had been sent to Manila to trade for silver, and it was
feared that an expedition would spoil the profits. Only 600 out of
the 2,000 sepoys promised were sent to the ships, and of their
quality Draper had no good to say. 'Such a Bandetti', he com-
plained, 'never assembled since the time of Sparticus.' Fortunately,
the company's military officers escaped his censure.

Cornish decided to risk French activity in Indian waters during

his absence further east, leaving only three ships behind him when the expedition sailed from Madras. The fleet consisted of eight ships of the line, three frigates, and three East India Company's vessels. Cornish flew his flag in HMS *Norfolk*, 74 guns. The second senior officer was Commodore Richard Tiddeman. He had his broad pendant in HMS *Elizabeth*, a third-rate of 64 guns, nearly 60 years old. Among captains of note were the elder Hyde Parker, commanding the *Grafton*, and Richard King, of the frigate *Argo*, both to make names for themselves in future wars. Cornish's nephew, Samuel Pitchford, who later took his uncle's name, commanded the *America*, 60 guns.

The number of troops was small. There were Draper's own regiment, which was well under strength; some gunners, European and Indian; the 600 sepoys: two companies of French deserters, native soldiers of doubtful quality; and some lascars as labourers. This made up a total of something over 1,700 men, to which could be added such marines as could be spared from the ships. Strength ruled out any possibility of a protracted siege, which would have required many more men. Draper based his hopes on the effects of bombardment from the sea, or a surprise landing, or a combination of the two.

'Perhaps the appearance of 7 or 8 line of battle ships may save us the trouble and Bloodshed of an attack,' he wrote home, 'but if not we shall begin directly with the Port of Cavita, as that must be our first object. The Great Ships can come near enough to batter it. We shall make an effort at the same time with the land forces; carry it we will, or perish in the attempt.' He concluded in a high strain: 'Living or dying I will endeavour to meet your Approbation.'

In order to ensure secrecy the frigate *Seahorse* commanded by Captain Grant, a veteran of Quebec, had been sent forward on 19 July to cruise in the Singapore Straits and to sever communications with Manila. Three days before Cornish sailed with the bulk of the fleet, on 1 August 1762, five ships were despatched under Tiddeman. He was to call at Malacca to request water from the Dutch governor, so as to shorten the time before the force could get clear of Singapore.

During the evening of 23 September the fleet, after negotiating the difficult passage through the Singapore Straits, sailed into Manila Bay and anchored near the subsidiary fortress of Cavita, where the Spanish dockyard was situated. No naval opposition was expected, and none was met with. It was too dark for bombardment, but during the night Cornish sent a number of sailing-masters to survey the shore and to prospect for suitable landing-places, bearing in mind the considerable surf which – as at Madras – could make disembarkation dangerous. The reports were satisfactory. Meanwhile Archbishop Rojo, the Spanish Governor and Captain-General, sent a note to the *Norfolk* demanding to know Cornish's business and whether any of his ships were in distress. Cornish and Draper replied jointly, giving Rojo formal notification of war with Spain and summoning him to surrender. Rojo refused.

The Spaniards had numbers on their side, 556 Europeans, 400 militiamen, and a force of Filipinos which would have made up a total of about 10,000 defenders. The town, with its outworks and fortifications, had elaborate protection, mainly from the landward side, but the guns were mounted on poor carriages. The streets and tracks were so rough that, the carriages being in a bad state, it would have been difficult to move batteries from place to place should this be necessary.

As surprise had been achieved and as the wind was unfavourable for an attack on Cavita, it was decided to assault Manila without preliminaries. Cavita would fall of itself once the town was in British hands. The chosen landing-place was opposite a church called the Malata, about a mile to the south of the town. The boat parties were under Colonel Monson, who commanded the left. Colonel Draper had the centre, and Major More the right. Monson's force was the real threat; Draper and More were to make feints to disperse the opposition. The longboats, each equipped with a 6-pounder gun, were in charge of Hyde Parker, Kempenfelt and William Brereton of the *Falmouth*, frigates giving covering fire. In spite of surf which filled or overturned several boats, a lodgement was made without loss of life. The first wave consisted of the 79th Regiment, marines, and artillerymen serving two field pieces.

Reinforcement continued throughout the night of 24 September and during the following day. The troops took possession of a powder store which Draper established as a position from which to cover the landing of stores. Colonel Monson occupied the Hermita, a church 900 yards from the walls of the town, and this served as general headquarters. Another officer, Captain Fletcher, occupied the church of Santiago, which was nearer the sea and within 300 yards of the Plaza, at a point where any breach of the outworks would have to be made. These dispositions were all the more valuable as giving shelter from the monsoon, which now became a threat, making the surf additionally hazardous and leading to some loss of life from drowning.

By 26 September Cornish decided that he could spare seamen

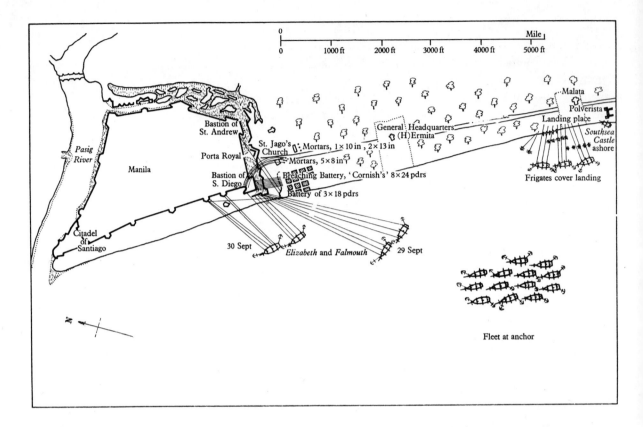

Siege of Manila

as well as marines for the land operations, and 700 were sent ashore. The same day the Spaniards, who were alarmed at the loss of the church of Santiago, made a sortie. This was led by a Frenchman, the Chevalier Faillet, who had under him about 400 men and two field pieces. The attack was repulsed by the men of the 79th Regiment and a hundred sailors under Colonel Monson, one of the Spanish guns being taken. Elated by this success, Draper sent another summons to Archbishop Rojo who once more replied 'No surrender'.

At this stage, there was a diversion. A galley was driven ashore by the navy, and the officers were taken prisoner. They proved to be from the galleon *Filipino*, which was reported to be on a course for Manila with a cargo of silver. Word flew round the fleet, memories of the *Cabadonga* were revived, and Cornish ordered the frigate *Argo* and the *Panther*, of 60 guns, to intercept her. It was also agreed that all prizes and plunder should be shared between the navy and army. Unfortunately, winds prevented the ships from sailing before 4 October, and meanwhile there was the problem of the prisoners. One of them was Rojo's nephew, Antonio Tagle, who was accommodated in the *Norfolk*. A truce was arranged to take him to his uncle, but this was broken owing to the indiscipline of some sepoys and Filipinos. Tagle was killed in attempting to save the life of his escort.

By 30 September preparations were nearing completion for battering the walls of Manila and making a breach, in which overwhelming naval gunfire would play a role. One ship employed in the work, the store carrier *Southsea Castle*, drove ashore in the rough weather. This, however, proved to be an advantage. When the sea went down, stores and guns could be put on shore without the use of boats, and by mounting guns on the decks of the stranded vessel, they could be used with more effect than those of ships anchored at a distance.

A second and fiercer counter-attack, in which Filipinos played a conspicuous part, was made on 4 October in a storm of rain. Draper wrote that if the Filipinos' 'Skill or Weapons had been equal to their Strength and Ferocity, it might have cost us dear. Altho' armed chiefly with Bows, Arrows and Lances, they advanced up to the very muzzles of our Pieces, repeated their Assaults, and died like wild Beasts, gnawing the Bayonets.' The British lost sixteen or seventeen men in this fracas.

By this time the Chevalier Faillet, convinced of the futility of continued resistance, advised Rojo to give in. The archbishop was persuaded to agree after an interview with Draper under a flag of truce. The formal surrender of the town took place on 5 October, one of the conditions being a ransom of $4 million. Draper promised that the inhabitants should continue to manage their own affairs without interference. The garrison then began to settle in. The troops put the citadel into a better state than it had ever been before.

On 10 October seamen and marines from the *Norfolk* and the frigate *Seahorse* went ashore at Cavita. The defenders did not wait for an attack, but either mutinied, surrendered, or ran off, arms in hand, after plundering whatever they could carry. The arsenal fell into British hands intact. Everything was found to facilitate a complete overhaul of the British ships. Kempenfelt was appointed Governor, and under his direction work proceeded apace. He was later sent home with despatches.

Manila fell owing to the weight of artillery bombardment, most of which was naval. The biggest guns, 24-pounders, fired 2,244 rounds, and 34,600 pounds of gunpowder were expended. By contrast, and largely in consequence, the cost in life and limb was light. Four military officers were killed and six were wounded. Commodore Tiddeman was accidentally drowned just after the assault was over, his boat overturning in the surf. The European casualties comprised 21 soldiers killed and 69 wounded; 5 sepoys were killed and 23 wounded. It was a small 'butcher's bill' for so complete a success.

The ransom was never paid. As a result, a great deal of prize-money was lost. The proceedings with Rojo were conducted by Draper in Latin. Cornish, in his rough-and-ready way, later declared he would never again accept a command in conjunction with a classical scholar, so disappointed was he at the outcome. Ransom apart, the conquest was of little value to Britain and no attempt was made to settle at Mindanao.

Manila was returned to Spain at the peace settlement, but there was little rejoicing at Madrid for the islands were in a state of ferment; guerrilla warfare was a regular feature of Philippine life. The British garrison, in two years' acquaintance, made no impression on the population and indeed their influence never extended beyond the capital. The connection was so brief that it comes as a surprise to many Americans to learn that they were not the first white people, after the Spaniards, to exercise authority there.

Although there was no repetition of the fantastic haul made by Anson, the commanders did well for themselves. Cornish felt able to accept a baronetcy a few years after his return to England, which argued easy circumstances; a single prize laid the foundation of at least one other naval fortune, that of the Hyde Parkers.

Antonio Tagle and the others captured in the galley late in September did not know that after they had left the galleon *Filipino* she had been damaged in a storm and had taken shelter in a little-known harbour at Samar. Captain King of the *Argo* and Hyde Parker, transferred to the *Panther*, might have gone off on a wild goose chase, but for an exceptional piece of luck. Another galleon was on the same course as the *Filipino* and it was she that was sighted by the look-outs on board the *Argo* on 30 October.

The larger *Panther* had been driven among the Ladrones by a current and nearly wrecked, but the *Argo*, despite having only 28 guns, and only 80 men at quarters, at once gave chase. Captain King soon closed with the enemy and began a spirited engagement as soon as he was within range. The frigate's armament made little impression on the thick sides of the galleon, and it was not until Parker had worked clear of the islands and arrived to King's assistance that the Spaniards surrendered. Great was the surprise of the British captains to learn that she was not the *Filipino*, but a ship of the size of a British first-rate of 100 guns. She was pierced for 60 guns but had only 13 mounted, 7 of which had been taken out of the hold during the course of the action, proof enough of how safe the 810 men on board considered themselves to be. In this respect the encounter was on a par with that of Anson's *Centurion* and the *Cabadonga*.

The galleon's name was the *Santissima Trinidada*, and her cargo was of enormous value, though not much of it was bullion. Some accounts say that it amounted to at least £500,000. King and Parker naturally benefited, and as Parker had his son serving as his first-lieutenant (nepotism being rife in the eighteenth-century navy), considerable reward accrued to the pair. The younger Hyde Parker was to continue to be lucky in the matter of prize.

Captain King, a particularly gallant officer, might have done even better, for Cornish sent him, in charge of his own ship and the *Seaford*, to search for and take possession of the *Filipino*. Some idea of the weather and other difficulties may be gathered from the fact that in spite of every incentive, financial and otherwise, King had to return empty-handed after a three months' search, his ship much the worse for wear, and his provisions nearly all gone. He succeeded to the command of the *Grafton*, and it was in this ship that he sailed back to England, escorting the *Santissima Trinidada*, the splendid vessel he had done so much to secure.

6 Two Battles off Cape St Vincent

Both before and after the capture of Manila, Spain was a 'soft option' for the Royal Navy. The country usually entered upon a war with Britain at the behest of France, or in her interests, and suffered accordingly. Her shipwrights continued to produce what British captains called 'Spanish beauties'. With some regularity they fell into unfriendly hands, as did a proportion of the silver of the New World which the Indians mined so unwillingly for their masters. Two particular occasions when the Spaniards came off worst took place near Cape St Vincent.

Thrusting out from the Portuguese coast so majestically, and set geographically between the estuary of the Tagus and the great Spanish port of Cadiz, with the castle of Sagres nearby (from which Prince Henry the Navigator organised the pioneering exploration of the African route to the Far East), Cape St Vincent was a fitting background for such important actions.

The events were seventeen years apart, but they had three ingredients in common – they marked times of crisis in long and complex wars. The British fleets were in charge of admirals of eminent distinction, and there could be no argument over the magnitude of success. Rodney's victory of 1780 was concerned with the relief of Gibraltar, which was then at the outset of the most severe of its various sieges. Jervis's victory of 1797, which like Rodney's took place during the winter season, gave the first opportunity for Nelson to show his tactical genius in battle. It also marked one of the various turning-points in the struggle with Napoleon. Rodney had superior strength. Jervis was faced with numbers so preponderant that had the Spaniards known their business he would have been crushed. The battles were so different and had such points of interest that it is odd they should ever be confused.

The trouble in 1780 arose from the war with the American colonists, which had begun five years earlier and was further than ever from a settlement. France had thrown her weight into the scales, hoping to regain some of the prestige she had lost as a result of the Seven Years' War. Spain had joined France because she had long-standing causes of resentment and pre-eminently because she wished to recapture Gibraltar, which had been ceded to Britain at the Treaty of Utrecht in the time of Queen Anne. She might have succeeded but for the sustained defence under General Eliott, later Lord Heathfield, who depended on the navy to run supplies through before starvation reduced him. This was done three times, in operations which entailed the passage of convoys through 'uncommanded seas', that is to say with enemies in potential strength along the line of passage. On the first occasion the feat was achieved by Rodney. It was so decisive that it helped to account for the success of later reliefs under Admirals Darby and Howe.

Rodney, who was the son of a captain of marines, was at the time a man of over sixty with a reputation both for professional skill and for financial misfortune, largely due to the expenses of electioneering. He loved high life, and in spite of a succession of good appointments and a full share of prize-money, he was seldom free from pecuniary embarrassments. It was, in fact, owing to the difficulty of finding men competent enough to take charge of the country's principal fleets that he was considered for employment at all. He had been in Paris, evading his creditors, when his chances seemed brightest. This was because dissension in the navy, political and personal, had eliminated many of his rivals.

The admiral was enabled to return to England thanks to a loan from a French friend, the Marshal Biron. Before going to Rodney's help Biron consulted the Minister of Marine, de Maurepas, in case the act should be thought unpatriotic. The marshal must have been reassured by de Maurepas' astonishing remark that he did not think much of naval warfare. 'It's piff-poff on either side, and afterwards the sea is just as salt!' And this from the minister in charge of the second navy in Europe! Rodney somehow managed to find the money to repay the marshal as the foremost obligation on his return to London. He found lodgings in Cleveland Row, opposite St James's Palace, where he was not only safe from duns but close to the centre of affairs.

Rodney's appointment could not have pleased him more. It was as 'Commander-in-Chief of HM ships and vessels at Barbados and the Leeward Islands and the seas adjoining'. He knew the Caribbean well from earlier service, and his bodily infirmities were such that he welcomed a warmer climate even though it entailed great activity. Lord Sandwich, then at the head of the admiralty, was running a risk in appointing Rodney in any

Admiral Lord Rodney (1719–92) defeated the Spaniards off Cape St Vincent, 1780 *after Sir Joshua Reynolds* NPG

capacity. He arranged for him to take as his flag captain an unknown officer, Walter Young, who had been 14 years a lieutenant and had been serving in the transport agent's office at Deptford. Considering how jealously Rodney looked upon patronage, this was an extraordinary decision. Although justified by events, it indicated that Young was expected to keep an eye on his chief and to report back to the admiralty, which he duly did, ascribing much wisdom to his own conduct. Rodney's health was uncertain; it was mid-winter, and his responsibilities were great. Even so, he lacked nothing in self-confidence, although it was seventeen years since he had sailed in time of war and he had never yet commanded a fleet against an enemy.

He sailed from Spithead on Christmas Eve 1779, with his flag in the 90-gun *Sandwich* and urged on by a note from the 1st Lord, who had heard that Spanish activity was increasing. He had charge of 22 men-of-war and 18 transports, with another force to join at Plymouth. Some of the ships would return to the home station after the operation, when Rodney himself would stretch across the Atlantic with such vessels as had been assigned to him.

Almost at once he had to take to his cot with an attack of gout and gravel, but his brain was as keen as ever and at the outset luck was with him. On 7 January 1780 his look-outs caught sight of a Spanish convoy of 16 ships protected by 7 escorts, most of them small. Considering Rodney's strength, the issue was never in doubt. All were captured and some were at once taken into British service. The senior ship of the escort, the *Guipuscoano* of 64 guns, was re-christened *Prince William*. This was to celebrate the fact that George III's son, William Henry, was serving as a midshipman in the fleet. As the future King William IV, he was the last King of England to be in action at sea until George VI was present at Jutland as a young naval officer.

All this was fortunate enough and there were better if sterner things to come. On 16 January, in typical north-Atlantic weather, the leading ship, the *Bedford*, reported an enemy squadron in sight. It was about noon and by 2.30 pm, when it was clear that the Spaniards did not intend to stand and fight, Rodney signalled for a 'general chase', ships to engage 'to leeward of the enemy'. The admiral believed that, in certain circumstances, the leeward position was best. This was one of them, for it would prevent the Spaniards from steering for the protection of their own coast. By the state of the sea, it also gave some advantage to his gunners.

A chase was a captain's dream, for he was free to act on his own initiative in pursuit of a flying foe, and when the winter daylight faded he would have no signals to worry him. Hawke had been the great exponent of such tactics, and as Rodney would have recollected, the old warrior was still living. The last great fleet victory at sea, fought in the confined waters of Quiberon Bay in the 'Year of Victories', 1759, had been just such an action, and it was the climax of Hawke's career. Hawke's flag had flown that day from the *Royal George*, and it so happened that this great three-decker was with Rodney's fleet. She was one of three flagships, Rodney's *Sandwich* being the senior, Rear-Admiral Digby's *Prince George* and Rear-Admiral Ross's *Royal George* being the others. The *Royal George*, by then twenty-four years old, played her part in disabling the Spanish flagship in the night action about to begin. Less than three years later, her structure worn out, she sank at Spithead when preparing for another relief of Gibraltar, with Richard Kempenfelt and most of her ship's company.

Rodney's fleet in pursuit of the
Spanish at St Vincent, 1780
Francis Holman   NMMG

A chase was the sort of action in which the British not only
revelled but excelled. Even the coming of night, and the continuing violent weather, gave no check to the work of destruction.
There was a bright moon – another piece of luck for Rodney –
enough sea room, and most ships, many of them fresh from
docking, sailed well.

The opposing force, under Don Juan de Langara, consisted of 9
ships of the line and 2 frigates. As the pursuit was by 22 ships of
the line, including 3 three-deckers, de Langara did the only
sensible thing in the circumstances. He fled. He could not hope to
save all his ships, but one or two might escape.

It was still daylight, about 4 pm, when the *Edgar* came up with
the rear-most Spaniard, the 70-gun *Santo Domingo*, which was
limping along with a broken mainyard and no sails on her main-
mast. The *Edgar* gave her a broadside and then pressed on, after
which the enemy was attacked successively by the *Marlborough*,
Ajax and *Bienfaisant*. One hour after the first exchanges the *Santo
Domingo*, which was still banging away at her opponents, suddenly
blew up. Only one man, astride a piece of mast, survived the
blast and the winter sea.

Half an hour later the *Princessa* struck, after a succession of

The Spanish ship *Santo Domingo* blowing up during Rodney's victory off Cape St Vincent, 1780
Richard Paton   NMMG

assaults from the *Marlborough*, *Ajax*, *Montagu*, *Bedford* and *Bienfaisant*. Then, in the moonlight, the British came upon the 80-gun *Fenix*, wearing de Langara's flag. She was attacked by the *Defence*, *Montagu*, *Royal George* and *Bienfaisant*, but put up a good resistance until 8.30 pm, when she had had enough. Three more successes followed fairly swiftly: the *Diligente* fell to the *Montagu* at 9.15 pm, and the *San Eugenio* surrendered to the *Cumberland*, *Montagu* and *Terrible* at about 11 pm, but in so damaged a state that she drove ashore and became a total loss. The *San Julian* hauled down her colours at some time after midnight to the *Cumberland* and *Prince George*, but she too could not be prevented from driving ashore, where she was salvaged later.

So far Rodney himself, receiving reports in his cot from Captain Young, had not been in action. When he hoisted the signal to chase he had summoned the Master, Hiscutt, and said: 'this ship is not to pay any attention to the merchantmen or small ships of war. Lay me alongside the biggest ship you can, or the admiral, if there be one.' The action turned out rather oddly. The *Sandwich* came up with the 70-gun *Monarca* during the course of the night. This ship was being engaged by the frigate *Apollo*, commanded by Captain Philemon Pownall, to whom she had

89

struck. Not knowing this the gunners of the *Sandwich* applied themselves with a will, until a hail from across the water made Young realise what had happened.

By then, the victory was as complete as it would ever be. Rodney had captured 6 ships of the line, of which all but 2 remained in his hands. Another had sunk, and of de Langara's squadron only 2 ships of the line and 2 frigates remained. Rodney's private view was that even these might not have escaped if all his captains had obeyed his order to engage from the leeward position. For an officer rescued from debt and dug out of retirement, it was a splendid start, besides being a tonic to the government which had arranged his appointment. The war was going so badly at this stage that when news was received at home, the reaction was ecstatic. Rodney was voted a pension of £1,000 a year, which was doubled by order of George III. He was already a baronet, and the king signified his pleasure over the battle by making him an additional Knight of the Bath, with a star for his coat. It was some time before he was well enough to receive the tribute due to his success from those ashore, but when he felt able to land he stayed nearly three weeks.

Flying his flag from the *Panther* at Gibraltar was Vice-Admiral Robert Duff. As a young officer he had shown an ardent spirit in Hawke's fleet, but the years had done him no good. General Eliott had been disappointed at his lack of zeal, and when Rodney arrived many watched Duff's behaviour with interest, for the two were not friends. Years before, Duff had disdained to serve as Rodney's flag captain and the incident was not forgotten. However, Duff wanted to go home and Rodney could oblige him. Duff's whole attitude altered wonderfully when he realised this, and his courtesy towards Rodney would have amused anybody who had seen their previous correspondence. He got his way, and for his part Rodney took the opportunity to promote one of his captains, authorising him to fly a commodore's broad pendant. This annoyed the admiralty so much that they sent a frigate to recall him.

After his stay ashore, Rodney departed for his proper station where he was to endure considerable frustration and, at the last, to gain much renown.

The situation of Sir John Jervis in 1797, as he cruised with his small fleet near the scene of Rodney's victory, could scarcely have been more different from that of his predecessor, and no one could have said that luck was with him. The success of French armies by land had driven the British from one position in the Mediterranean after another, until it had been abandoned. Jervis was based on Lisbon and Gibraltar, his force scarcely more than one of observation, so preponderant was Franco-Spanish strength. The old alliance of the two countries had revived, and once again Britain was hard pressed.

Rodney and Jervis were not dissimilar in age or character. Both were strict disciplinarians, entire masters of their business, and rightly confident in their own abilities. The difference was that Jervis was without Rodney's weaknesses, and that he had been on continuous active service since the outbreak of the war with France four years before. Among his achievements had been the capture of the French West Indian island of Martinique, in co-operation with the army, a feat which was a repetition of one by Rodney and General Monkton during the Seven Years' War.

Jervis's principal duty was to keep watch on Cadiz, to support the Portuguese (who were under threat of a Franco-Spanish invasion), to interrupt the coastal traffic on which, in the existing state of their roads, the Spaniards relied, and to abort the various schemes of attack on the British Isles, planned so often when France and Spain were at war with Britain, and attempted so seldom. Ireland was the target, and French and Spanish squadrons in Mediterranean ports had been ordered to concentrate at Brest. It was a bad season for operations, but the short hours of daylight gave every chance of evasion by commanders wishing to avoid action.

A French force did in fact sail from Toulon in mid-December 1796, and after passing through the Straits of Gibraltar made its way north. A few weeks later a Spanish fleet left Cartagena with the same intention, and with the immediate duty of escorting a convoy of mercury to Cadiz. The mercury came from mines at Almaden, 100 miles north of Malaga, the richest deposit in Europe. It was used to amalgamate the silver from the Spanish possessions in the New World, on which Spanish and French economy now largely depended. With cargoes of such value, a strong escort was essential.

The Spanish Admiral was de Corbova, and his force was so powerful that in size of ships it could not be matched by any existing navy. It included the huge *Santissima Trinidada*, the largest man-of-war afloat mounting 136 guns, and 6 other ships more heavily armed than any single vessel in the British fleet. The mercury was in 4 *urcas*, which were large merchantmen. Jervis, who never had a close sight of them and had no idea of the nature and importance of what they were carrying, thought them to be men-of-war.

Had it not been for his supreme confidence, Jervis could well have been shaken by successive blows which had befallen his ships. A few weeks before he met the Spaniards, he had been reduced to ten of the line by accidents mainly due to atrocious weather. The *Courageux*, dragging her anchors, had been driven out of Gibraltar Bay and wrecked on the African coast with heavy loss of life. The *Bombay Castle* ran on to a sandbank in the Tagus estuary, owing to a dearth of competent pilots. The *Gibraltar* (which was the name by which de Langara's *Fénix* of the 1780 battle had been rechristened when taken into British service) had driven ashore, though she was saved. The *Zealous*, also preserved by the skill of her ship's company, struck a rock in Tangier Bay and suffered considerable damage. Finally, the *St George* ran aground, and the *Meleager* was forced to return to Lisbon for repairs to her bowsprit.

Even before these discouraging events, Rear-Admiral Robert Man, who had been on duty off Cadiz with seven ships of the line, lost his nerve and with the concurrence of his captains returned precipitately to England, although everyone knew the straits to which Jervis was reduced. Heads should have fallen, but Jervis was understanding. He knew Man to be in ill-health and despondent, and that such an attitude was worse than useless in time of war. He wrote to Lord Spencer at the admiralty, 'when the Blue Devils prevail, there is an end to resource and energy. . . . I beg I may have no more admirals, unless they are firm men'.

Jervis's luck began to turn on 6 February, not a moment before he needed it. Five of the line under Sir William Parker joined him from England. Parker had his flag in the *Prince George*. A week later Commodore Nelson, his broad pendant flying from the frigate *Minerve*, gave Jervis the latest news of the enemy. Returning from a foray into the Mediterranean, he had sailed clean through the Spanish fleet during a fog which had lifted in time for him to make his escape without being detected, but with reliable information about de Cordoba's whereabouts and course. Nelson, who was a refreshment to any commander-in-chief, was ordered to transfer to the *Captain*. From what the commodore told him, Jervis knew that a battle was certain. He did not fear it, but he knew that the odds were against him and he had had little time to assure himself that Parker's ships were equal to the exceptional standards he demanded.

The enemy was sighted soon after dawn on Valentine's Day, 14 February 1797. 'A victory is very essential to England at this moment', Jervis was heard to say, and he signalled to that effect to the fleet. The Spaniards were about fifteen miles to the south-west. 'Thumpers,' recorded the signal lieutenant of the *Barfleur*, 'they loom like Beachy Head in a fog.'

As visibility increased, Sir Robert Calder, who was Jervis's Captain of the Fleet, viewed the size and numbers of the Spaniards with concern.

'There are eight sail of the line, Sir John', he reported.

'Very well, Sir.'

'There are twenty sail of the line, Sir John.'

'Very well, Sir.'

'There are twenty-seven sail of the line, Sir John, near double our number.'

'Enough, Sir', was the tart reply. 'No more of that: the die is cast; and if there are fifty sail of the line, I will go through them.'

Captain Hallowell, formerly of the *Courageux*, was on board Jervis's flagship, the *Victory*. Standing near the admiral he so far forgot himself in his delight at the reply that he clapped his commander-in-chief on the back, saying: 'That's right, Sir John: that's right! By God, we'll give them a damned good licking!'

For its size, 15 ships of the line and 4 frigates, Jervis's force was itself both powerful and highly experienced under war conditions. There were 4 flag officers including the commander-in-chief, each of them in three-decked ships. The newly joined commodore had a ship of 74 guns; and only one vessel, the *Diadem* of 64 guns, was less well-armed. In remarking to Calder that he would 'go through' the enemy, Jervis was being precise. It was apparent that the Spaniards were in no sort of order, and in fact they had been carried into the Atlantic far beyond what the admiral could have intended. The wind was east-north-east, and de Cordoba was intent on making his way to Cadiz at his best speed.

The Spaniards were in two distinct groups, one of which was to windward of Jervis, with another, containing the *urcas*, some way to leeward. Jervis, approaching from the north in two columns abreast, ordered a line ahead and steered for the gap between the two divisions of the enemy, thus separating them more firmly than ever. His intention was to alter course in succession when the manoeuvre was complete, and then to attack the larger group. His action caused some confusion among the enemy, but Jervis may have left the executive signal for the new course a shade too late – the matter being difficult to judge since on this occasion the *Victory* was not leading the fleet. Although it was clear that the foremost ships would soon be among the enemy as intended, shortly before 1 pm when the light was as

Admiral Lord St Vincent (1735–1823) defeated the Spaniards off Cape St Vincent, 1797 *portrait from the studio of Lemuel Abbott* NPG

good as it ever would be that day, Nelson perceived that the leading Spanish ships, which included some of the largest, were likely to escape. They were beginning to pass astern of the British line, which, under the eye of a martinet, was turning in the exact order prescribed from the *Victory*.

The *Captain* happened to be the rear ship but two. The *Diadem* followed her and then the *Excellent*, the latter ship commanded by Nelson's close friend, Cuthbert Collingwood. On his own initiative, Nelson gave orders for the *Captain* to wear out of the line and to head straight for the leading Spaniards. It was an action of which few other officers would have been capable, and it was followed later by Collingwood, who had the same tactical perception. Nelson had been in fleet actions before, but in his view they had been imperfectly conducted. He did not intend to be robbed on this occasion of what he knew to be a priceless opportunity, one of those 'lucky moments in war' which, according to one of his heroes, James Wolfe, lead on to fortune. His instinct was right.

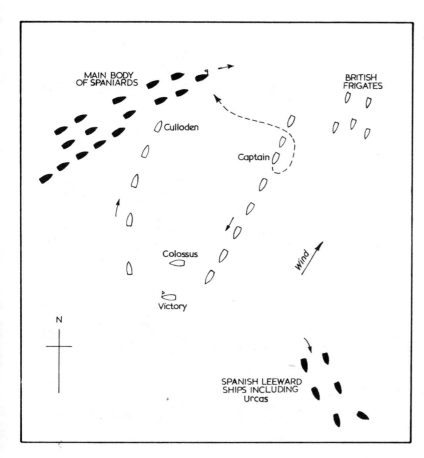

The rest of the day proved as melodramatic as anything in naval history. Although at risk of being blown out of the water by the combined broadsides of the *Santissima Trinidada, San Josef* and *Salvador del Mundo*, the ships he steered for, Nelson's move forced the Spaniards to alter course; and soon the *Captain, Excellent* and *Culloden*, the latter of which was at the head of Jervis's line, were in the thick of it. The *Culloden* was commanded by Thomas Troubridge, Jervis's favourite captain. These three ships, together with the three-decker *Prince George* and the *Blenheim*, under Captain Frederick, had the hottest work. All the rest did well except for the unhappy *Colossus* which, besides being structurally defective, lost her fore top-sail yard. Her Captain, George Murray, could take only a distant part in what turned into the sort of *mêlée* customary in the old wars with the Dutch, and much to the mind of most British officers.

After being an hour in action, during which time it was evident that they were under-manned and had poorly trained crews, the *Salvador del Mundo*, 112 guns, and the *San Ysidro*, 74 guns, struck

General engagement at the Battle of
St Vincent, 1797   *Thomas Luny*
NMMG

their colours. It was thought that the *Santissima Trinidada* did the same to Captain Saumarez of the *Orion*, but before a prize crew could take possession she escaped in the confusion of the later afternoon. Then the damaged *San Josef*, 112 guns, and the *San Nicholas*, 80 guns, ran foul of one another, enabling Nelson to board them from the *Captain* as they drifted interlocked. This was a personal exploit in the manner of a story by Marryat or Forester. Nelson composed his own account of it all, which he took trouble to ensure had a wide circulation.

The battle ended during the later afternoon and de Cordoba, having lost four ships, showed no eagerness to renew fighting next day. He withdrew to Cadiz where the leeward group of Spanish ships, including the consignment of mercury, arrived quickly. The *Santissima Trinidada*, well escorted, was nearly three weeks at sea under a jury rig before she found sanctuary at Algeçiras. The British casualties were astonishingly light. Between them the *Captain, Blenheim, Excellent, Prince George* and *Culloden* had 65 killed, against a total of 8 for all the rest of the fleet.

Jervis was given an earldom in recognition of his victory. It

Nelson boarding the *San Nicholas* at
the Battle of St Vincent, 1797
F. S. Baden-Powell
Walker Art Gallery, Liverpool

came at a time of deep gloom when the Bank of England had suspended cash payments, and when affairs were such that when news from the fleet first arrived the party bearing Jervis's despatches had difficulty in raising a few pounds-worth of credit to meet the expense of the road journey to London. It was noted that the admiral was raised three steps in the peerage at one bound, but the reason for this was that the king had decided earlier that he should have a barony and it was at the royal behest that he took the title of St Vincent. Rodney, who might also have had a claim to it, had been dead some years and there was indeed no comparison between the merits of the two actions. Parliament added a pension of £3,000 a year to support the title.

Nelson, who reached Rear-Admiral's rank by seniority six days after the battle, was made a Knight of the Bath, the distinction to which he aspired and in which he took the greatest pleasure. He enjoyed being a hero, and liked people to know him as such. There were, however, those in the fleet, and they included Sir William Parker, who resented his self-advertisement. Even Saumarez, who was was slightly his junior, made an ironic allusion to 'our desperate Commodore'. Sir Robert Calder, not noted for generosity of spirit towards comrades-in-arms, remarked to Jervis that Nelson had disregarded orders during the course of the action. 'It certainly was so,' replied Jervis, 'and if you ever commit such a breach of your orders, I will forgive you also.'

Apart from the *Prince George*, which was present and took a noteworthy part at both battles of St Vincent, there was an eye-witness to the aftermath of Rodney's victory and of the entire course of Jervis's. This was a soldier, John Drinkwater, once of the Royal Manchester Volunteers. He had served under General Eliott throughout the great siege of Gibraltar, of which he published an account, and was thus able to witness the rejoicings at the arrival of Rodney.

During Jervis's battle he was a passenger on board the frigate *Lively*, Captain Lord Garlies. It was in his *Narrative* that some of the most characteristic glimpses of Nelson were first set down, for the two were friends as well as great admirers of the commander-in-chief. Drinkwater, who lived to be eighty-two, later changed his name to Bethune, and in his later years had the happiness to see a second edition of his work called for. The fame of Rodney and Jervis endured, but Nelson continued to be *news*.

Nelson receiving the surrender of the *San Nicholas* at the Battle of St Vincent, 1797   *Richard Westall* NMMG

7 Breaking the Line: Rodney off Dominica

Rodney's most resounding feat came more than two years after his moonlight battle – he saved Jamaica from invasion and won a victory over the Comte de Grasse in the Saints Passage, a channel which lies between Dominica and Guadeloupe.

The importance of the command which Rodney took up in the Leeward Islands was next to that of the home fleet, and of squadrons operating off the coast of North America. For generations France and Britain had struggled for power in the West Indies, each successive war being the occasion of local invasion and counter-invasion and of a struggle for dominance in the whole area of the Caribbean.

Both countries had acquired a share of the islands, from which enormous wealth in produce was sent back to Europe. The struggle seems to have been symbolised in the history of St Christopher's, usually known as St Kitts, which Rodney was concerned to protect. In the reign of James I, a Suffolk squire, Sir Thomas Warner, became the first English settler. In due time he was buried in a dignified tomb which still survives. The French, who arrived within a few years, attempted to oust him. More than once, at later stages, they got complete possession of the island. They did not keep it.

On his arrival in the Caribbean, Rodney found jaded captains, not uplifted by the general course and conduct of the war with the American colonists. In a personal way, it was no happy band of brothers. Rodney himself did not work by gentle persuasion and his uncertain health, together with his stern way of looking at things, was unlikely to increase what little harmony existed. His adversary was at first the Comte de Guichen, an experienced officer who had a powerful fleet at his disposal, and a more active disposition than many French admirals with whom he had crossed swords.

So far as naval resources were concerned, the most important French island was Martinique. It was there that de Guichen had his headquarters. The British had captured nearby St Lucia, but their richest possession, apart from Jamaica away to the west, was Barbados. It was de Guichen's intention to take this island by a powerful combined operation, and the opening moves of Rodney's cruise were designed to prevent this. Rodney succeeded, as the result of an action fought on 17 April 1780. This took place before he had been able to imbue his captains with his notion of concentrating his main force on part of the enemy's line, instead of fighting in the rigid and all too often unsatisfactory way of ship to ship.

Although strategically the action achieved its purpose and the *Sandwich* covered herself with glory, Rodney was furious with his subordinate admirals, Hyde Parker the elder and Joshua Rowley, for not carrying out his intentions. He actually suspected some captains of disaffection, not merely of what he thought stupidity. When the fleet returned to harbout, his remarks were vitriolic. He considered that the flag, meaning the *Sandwich*, had not been properly supported and he wrote to Rowley to say that 'the painful task of thinking belongs to me'.

Right in principle as Rodney was, if he had been able to make his thoughts as clear to others as they seemed to himself he might have won another victory to follow the winter triumph over the Spaniards. As it was, a succession of duels with the wary and experienced de Guichen left everything tactically undecided during Rodney's early months of command. The British position in the West Indies was not improved. and another season had to be awaited before matters could mend. In the West Indies the wind decided strategy to a greater extent than in almost any other area. A constant factor was the trade wind blowing in from the Atlantic from the north-east. From May until October it veers round almost to due east, and during the last few months of this period the advent of hurricanes made general campaigning impracticable.

Rodney went to North America for the hurricane season of 1780, much to the chagrin of the local Admiral, Marriott Arbuthnot. On his return to the Caribbean the next event which stirred him, and was a source of trouble for the rest of his life, was his capture of the Dutch island of St Eustatius, close by St Kitts. This was a result of the entry of Holland into the war alongside the French and Spanish in support of the Americans.

St Eustatius was an *entrepôt*, a storehouse on a huge scale from which goods of every kind (naval material included) could be supplied to both sides. Rodney was convinced that the action of English merchants who made use of the island was traitorous. This reason, added to the prospect of a windfall in prize-money, caused the affairs of the island to occupy him more than they should have done. That, at any rate, was the view of Sir Samuel Hood, another appointment to Rodney's fleet which was almost as odd as that of his flag captain.

Hood, who happened to be an old acquaintance of Rodney, had taken a shore job and had not expected to see further active service. But he was able and ambitious, and when the chance came to go to sea in an important post he was not reluctant. He was specially promoted to the flag list and went off to the West Indies in high expectation. He had moments of brilliance as a tactician and he was later praised, perhaps over-praised, by Nelson. But he could be as acidulent as his commander-in-chief, and he lacked Rodney's occasional compensating generosity. When Rodney first heard of Hood's advent, he wrote privately that 'they might as well send me an old applewoman'. This was an uninhibited expression, and there is no doubt that Rodney did not expect as much from Hood as Hood could give.

Hood joined Rodney in time to take part in events at St Eustatius at the end of January 1781. He was then sent to blockade Martinique, and was of the opinion that the disposition of his ships, as ordered by Rodney, prevented his interception of de Grasse, who arrived in April 1781 bringing with him a force superior in numbers. He then joined Rodney in Antigua, to find his commander-in-chief preparing to sail home before the onset of the hurricane season. Rodney was seething with indignation at the merchants, and regardless of what capacity they might have to harass him by means of actions at law for seizure of their property.

Hood next sailed for North American waters, and was present at the crucial Battle of the Chesapeake, fought in September. Admiral Thomas Graves, who was senior to Hood, failed to defeat de Grasse, partly because of Hood's rigid obedience in keeping to a strict line of battle when a stroke of initiative would have made all the difference. The failure made inevitable the surrender of an army which was at Yorktown under General Cornwallis. The disaster did not actually conclude the war, but it signified that the British had lost it and for once sea power had failed her. Moreover, de Grasse, fortified by a success which had cost him so little and gained so much, now planned large-scale operations in the West Indies. They would include an invasion of Jamaica, in which he could have relied on the help of a Spanish contingent.

At the stage when Rodney was about to be reunited with his command, having recovered his health and made a fast passage from England, Hood was at St Kitts. This island had been invaded by the French in superior numbers, and they were pressing the defences. Hood could not redeem the situation, though he added to his fame as a tactician by seizing the French anchorage and repelling all attempts to dislodge him. He was, however, in the position of being blockaded, and was only able to rejoin Rodney by cutting his cables at night and sailing away under de Grasse's nose. The military defence collapsed soon after his retreat.

Another crisis had by now been reached, and the scene was set for a decisive action such as Rodney had been awaiting for more than two years. He himself behaved with renewed vigour and showed exceptional civility to Hood, who was feeling the effects of many months of tension, by paying a call on him in the *Barfleur*. He stayed for two hours, discussing matters more amicably than had often been his way.

Rodney now had thirty-six of the line at his command, and from his station at Castries, St Lucia, he kept ceaseless watch on French preparations at Fort Royal, Martinique, by means of frigates. He intended to intercept de Grasse before the French could join forces with the Spaniards, who were making ready at San Domingo.

On 8 April Rodney received news that the French had weighed anchor. He put to sea and gave chase. Next day the fleets made contact at dusk, near Dominica, but lay-to for the night. When daylight came, de Grasse's fleet and his convoy were at first becalmed under the lee of the land, but the van under Vaudreuil managed to catch some wind in the channel north of the island. When Rodney tried to close the enemy, he also found himself becalmed. Hood, however, aided by such light breezes as came his way, crept ever nearer to Vaudreuil and was in action by 9.0 am with nine ships.

de Grasse then ordered his convoy to make for Guadeloupe as best they could. He himself tried to work to windward, his purpose being to draw Rodney away from Hood. But the sight of Hood's division, outnumbered and unsupported by the main body of the British through lack of wind, was too great a temptation and de Grasse added his gunfire to that of his subordinate. Hood withstood the attack for four hours, but it was at long range and by not pressing his advantage de Grasse lost a great opportunity. Shortly after midday, Rodney found a wind and was able to go to Hood's support. Firing ceased soon afterwards, with no ships lost but casualties in Hood's division, including Captain Bayne of the *Alfred*. Rodney's new flagship, the *Formidable*, lost a lieutenant and four seamen.

Now that he had got to grips with de Grasse, Rodney did not intend to let him go. The French had a military convoy to consider, at present safe under the forts at Guadeloupe. The British were free to pursue. A slight advantage in numbers would be altered completely if de Grasse was able to join eighteen Spaniards at San Domingo. For three days the chase continued, though at a crawl, owing to light breezes.

The first misadventure occurred on the night of 10–11 April, when the *Zélé* of 74 guns collided with the *Caton*, which had to be sent to Guadeloupe for repairs. Next morning the *Zélé* and another Frenchman, damaged aloft, could be seen struggling to leeward of the French fleet, which forced the admiral to bear down to their aid. The luckless *Zélé* had a second collision the night after her first, this time with the French flagship. de Grasse himself was lucky to escape with minor damage, but he was forced to detach the *Zélé* to join the *Caton*.

At dawn on 12 April the fleets were within a few miles of each other, between the northern end of Dominica and the islets known as the Saints. de Grasse had lost much advantage in safeguarding the *Zélé*, and now had two courses open to him. He could run down to leeward towards the waiting Rodney, or turn on a southerly course and, while keeping the wind gauge, escape with possibly only a brush with the British. He chose the latter alternative as a full-scale fight was not his intention.

Rodney, for his part, ordered Hood's battered ships, which were in the van, to the rear of his line. Rear-Admiral Drake, in the *Princessa* which had been captured in the moonlight battle, took Hood's place with his fresh division. The manœuvre being completed smoothly, Rodney, his Captain of the Fleet (Sir Charles Douglas), his Flag Captain (Symons), who had replaced Young the previous year, the physician (Sir Gilbert Blane), and the Chaplain (William Pagett), sat down to breakfast. Lord Cranstoun, an officer of experience, remained on deck to watch the enemy's movements.

The group in the great cabin of the *Formidable*, eating their leisurely meal within sight of the French, included Blane and Douglas, two remarkable men. They spoke well for Rodney's judgement when this was unfettered. Blane, a disciple of James Lind, had greatly improved the health record of the fleet, particularly by his insistence on the use of proper anti-scorbutics and by his ideas on ventilation. Rodney, who suffered many ills, was spared the horrors of scurvy, for Blane ensured that he had plenty of lemons. Sir Charles Douglas was a gunnery expert who had made the *Formidable* as efficient a ship as the navy possessed,

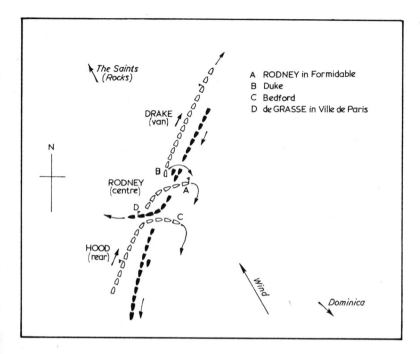

A RODNEY in Formidable
B Duke
C Bedford
D de GRASSE in Ville de Paris

The Saints
(Rocks)

DRAKE
(van)

N

RODNEY
(centre)

HOOD
(rear)

Wind

Dominica

improving the traverse of the guns and replacing the clumsy powder horns used for firing with tin boxes and quills.

During the early hours of 12 April, the van of the two lines of ships began to creep towards each other – de Grasse because he could not help it, Rodney by design. They were on opposite tacks, with the wind abeam. As they grew closer it was apparent that although the van ships were sailing as near the wind as possible, de Grasse would keep the advantage of the weather gauge.

As early as 7.30 am the leading French ships began to fire at long range. Captain Penny of the *Marlborough*, leading the British line, withheld fire until within 400 yards of the French. His broadside was followed by those of the *Arrogant*, *Alcide*, *Nonsuch*, *Conqueror*, *Princessa*, *Prince George* (always in the thick of it), *Torbay*, *Anson*, *Fame* and *Russell*. The *Russell* had the luckiest captain in either fleet. James Saumarez, from a well-known Channel Island family, had recently exchanged from a frigate into a ship of the line by leave of Hood, because her captain wished to return home. Saumarez was in action ten minutes after the *Marlborough*.

The *Formidable* and the centre division began to engage shortly after 8 am, when cannon smoke began to obscure the movements of individual ships and it became a case of follow-my-leader. One by one the French ships slipped past, and Rodney's main idea was to contract his own line and to close the range as much as he could. He signalled for his ships to alter course towards the enemy, and there was no holding back. It was an opportunity for which most captains had waited impatiently for years. At 8.30 am Captain Blair of the *Anson* was killed, and the *Marlborough*, having reached the head of the French line, hove-to in order to repair damage. The French employed their usual practice of firing high in order to hit masts, spars, sails and rigging, and thus cripple an opposing ship rather than inflict losses on her men.

The lines were so protracted, with 36 British and 30 French ships, that it was 9.25 am before Hood's flagship, the *Barfleur*, fired her guns. Rodney had backed the *Formidable*'s topsails to prolong his exchange with the much larger *Ville de Paris*, and was nearing the last ships of the French centre. Then came a shift in the wind from a steady breeze from east-south-east to light and variable winds from nearer south. This signified a crisis for de Grasse. His line, never well-drilled, fell into confusion; ships fouled each other and fell away to leeward. A gap opened near the advancing *Formidable* which had already been made use of by the *Duke*, whose Captain Gardner at first trembled for his head until, with infinite relief, he saw his commander-in-chief behind him.

The first victim was the *Glorieux*, 74 guns, which passed so near the *Formidable* that Rodney ordered the muzzles of the guns to be fully depressed. The *Namur* continued execution, so did Cornwallis in the *Canada*, by which time the Frenchman's masts had toppled over the side, her guns were silent, and she lay still in the water. By 9.15 am the *Formidable* was through the gap, and she was followed by the *Namur*, *St Albans*, *Canada*, *Repulse* and *Ajax*. The French line was well and truly broken. Credit for the step would be claimed by many, including the partisans of a certain Mr John Clerk of Eldin, a Scots amateur writer on naval tactics.

Contemporaries spoke of the course of the *Duke*, *Formidable* and other ships as an 'incision', which indeed it was, made possible by a fluke of wind. Lord St Vincent, a realist, summed the matter up in a few words: 'Rodney passed through the enemy's line by accident, not design, although historians have given him credit for the latter.' If this was the truth, it did not detract from Rodney's achievement, which could only have been spoilt by superior discipline and gunnery on the part of the French. This they did not possess.

de Grasse now had no choice but to abandon the *Glorieux* and to run before such wind as there was. Any hope he may have

nurtured of an operation against Jamaica vanished, and his need was to save as much of his fleet as he could.

The Battle of the Saints, 1782. Surrender of the French flagship
Thomas Luny   NMMG

The task was made easier by Rodney who, with many of his ships repairing damage, was in no hurry to order a general chase although the day was still before him. He commanded an orderly pursuit, not realising the state of the enemy. This infuriated Hood – but by 3 pm the British van and centre had come up with the French rear, which caused some of the bolder ships of the French centre to put about in support. The action cost de Grasse the loss of the *César*, *Hector* and *Ardent* of 64 guns, the latter of which had been taken from the British three years earlier off Plymouth.

Four captures was creditable, although no great matter under the circumstances. There was better to come. The *Ville de Paris* was in trouble, and she was deserted by the nearest ships. One of these, the *Auguste*, was commanded by Bougainville, the circumnavigator who had played a leading part the previous year at the Chesapeake.

By 6 pm the French flagship was under fire from the *Marlborough*, *Barfleur* and *Russell*. Hood fired one last broadside, and down came de Grasse's flag from the main top-masthead. It was 6.30 pm and Rodney, to Hood's chagrin, then made the signal for the fleet to break off action and lie to. Commodore Edmund Affleck in the *Bedford* did in fact hold on his course until 3 am, but in the morning light he could see no sign of the French. Rodney was far away to the rear, dazzled at having the tall and chivalrous de Grasse a prisoner on board the *Formidable*.

Owing to carelessness at some time during the hours of darkness, the *César* perished by fire and explosion, with the loss of 400 Frenchmen and a lieutenant and prize crew of 58 seamen from the *Centaur*. Hood came on board the *Formidable* at first light to pay his respects, and to urge a hot pursuit. He was greeted with words which filled him with anger and depression, as they did Nelson on a similar occasion during the following decade. 'Come,' said Sir George to Sir Samuel, 'we have done very handsomely as it is.'

Hood was silent, venting his wrath later on Sir Charles Douglas, who was his junior. The truth was that Rodney was old, and strained, and tired. He was somewhat bemused by the enormous size of the *Ville de Paris*, with her 104 guns and her stately build. One of his midshipmen, Joseph Yorke, aged fourteen and a connection of Anson's, wrote to his uncle, Lord Hardwicke: 'Sir Charles Douglas went on board of her and said that the *Formidable* was a bum-boat to her.' Rodney wrote to Philip Stevens, the Secretary of the Admiralty, reporting 'a most Complete Victory' and praising everyone, Hood in particular. This was exaggeration, as only four ships had survived capture and the French flagship herself was to perish in a storm on her way back to England, along with other ships of the line suffering from poor or damaged masts.

Hood had a small consolation, which he richly deserved. Eight days later, off Porto Rico, the *Caton* and the *Jason*, knowing nothing of the battle, had the mischance to fall in with his division which was once again ahead of the fleet. Both ships had had damage patched up at Guadeloupe, and they were an easy prey. With them were taken the frigate *Aimable* of 32 guns and the sloop *Ceres*, another ship once British.

The action off Dominica was as decisive strategically as that of the action two years earlier, in that French plans had been foiled. Rodney at last dominated the Caribbean, and the war at sea ended with an event creditable to the Royal Navy, which had been in adversity so long.

At home, the ministry which had chosen Rodney had fallen.

Model of proposed statue to Admiral
Rodney for Jamaica   *John Bacon*
Victoria & Albert Museum

Sandwich's successor at the admiralty recalled him, sending an undistinguished officer to replace him. News of the success came just too late to cancel the change, though every effort was made to do so. The newly arrived Admiral, Hugh Pigot, was followed by news of the bestowal of peerages on Rodney and Hood. Rodney would return a national hero, whatever ministry happened to be in power.

He lived for ten more years, never affluent, for the business of St Eustatius went against him. He had to be content with honour, glory and a modest income. He died in May 1792 shortly before another long war began, during the course of which many of his captains would gain distinction.

A small matter which would have given him great satisfaction – since he liked recognition to be given where appropriate – was that a line regiment, later to become known as the Welch Regiment, acquired a battle honour for their colours, a naval crown superscribed '12 April 1782'. This particular regiment supplied detachments for the fleets both of Rodney and, later, of St Vincent. It was the only one to be twice honoured for a share in naval victories.

There is a certain waywardness about memorials to some of the greater naval figures. Both Rodney and Hawke lie not in Westminster Abbey or St Paul's, but in two modest Hampshire churches – Hawke at North Stoneham and Rodney at Old Alresford. But Rodney's most elaborate commemoration was at Jamaica where settlers, relieved and elated at the Battle of the Saints, commissioned John Bacon to design a monument to stand at Spanish Town. Bacon's model, now in the Victoria & Albert Museum, showed the admiral in uniform, as he would certainly have preferred. The sculptor (at the behest of Sir Joshua Reynolds) changed all that. The testy old peer was transformed into a Roman in much the same odd way as George I appears – topping the steeple of St George's Church, Bloomsbury, with a lightning-conductor rising above his head.

8 Was the First of June So Glorious?

A well-connected young midshipman, Richard Howe, who in 1740 had sailed for the south Atlantic in Anson's expedition, survived into a very different era. Over the years he held, with credit, every rank in the service. Aside from this, he had a career in politics which brought him high office – Treasurer of the Navy, and, later, 1st Lord of the Admiralty.

Howe took part in four separate wars, in three of which he held important commands. This record has rarely been equalled and never surpassed. On Anson's voyage he was a junior, but he had risen to post captain's rank by the time of the Seven Years' War, during which, in certain operations, he was authorised to fly a commodore's broad pendant. In the War of American Independence he was commander-in-chief of the key area during the earlier stages of the conflict. Then, after a period of retirement, he had taken charge of the main fleet and brought relief to Gibraltar on the third and last occasion when it was necessary. Although this had led to no major encounter, Howe himself thought of it as the most difficult task he ever carried through.

When war opened with revolutionary France in 1793, Earl Howe, as he had by then become, was the doyen of sea officers. He was George III's favourite. The sovereign felt at ease when Howe was in charge of the fleet. He was authorised to fly the Union flag from the main top-masthead, in recognition of his unique services afloat and ashore. Into what better hands could the fleet be entrusted in days when Britain once more had to shoulder the burden of a maritime war? Whilst the king was in no doubt over the matter, Howe himself, who had pondered the characters and careers of his fellow-admirals as attentively as he had followed every tactical and technical development, considered that his age – which was sixty-seven – should have ruled him out. But there was no denying a monarch for whom he had the utmost veneration.

Professional opinion was entirely with the sovereign. There was no one with the variety of Howe's experience of war.

Admiral Lord Howe (1726–99)
J. S. Copley   NMMG

Although some of his juniors had reservations about his ability to inspire subordinates, a gift not given to all the abler tacticians, there were no two views about his being the best choice. Lord St Vincent, who was no hero-worshipper, remarked later: 'Lord Howe wore blue breeches, and I like to follow him even in my dress!' Nelson, sitting down to answer Howe's letter of congratulation after the Battle of the Nile, addressed him as 'the great, the immortal Earl Howe, our great Master in naval tactics and bravery'. If anyone could set the tone in the fleet for a struggle in which the more percipient could foresee might be protracted, it was the taciturn 'Black Dick', the nickname by which Howe was known to the sailors in reference to his swarthy complexion.

Howe never sought popularity, but he was trusted and respected. One of his defects, which it was sometimes remarked with a smile might have resulted from an early spell at Eton, was that although he had beautiful handwriting his style was obscure. The simplest statement would be expressed in convoluted prose. George III once wrote about whom he called, with affection, his *peculiar* admiral that he was 'not without much reserve, that at times do so envelope his meaning that it is not easy to bring him to the point'.

Happily, by means of a new signal-book which owed more to his efforts and those of Richard Kempenfelt than to any other factors, Howe could make his intentions better understood at sea than Rodney had ever done. He was as much of a disciplinarian as the older man, but his rebukes were never as stinging, for they were well wrapped up.

Although the revolutionaries in France had disposed of a large number of naval officers, many of whom had been drawn from aristocratic families, good work in reorganisation had been done in some of the ports, Brest in particular. The Royal Navy would have something to fight against, since energy and fanaticism had partly made up for the hereditary expertise on which seamen relied. As Howe was of a school of thought which differed from that of Anson and Hawke in that he considered close blockade by capital ships a wasteful policy, it was more than a year after war began before there was an action on any scale. So much so that Howe was at times referred to among the ignorant as 'Lord Torbay', deriving from a favourite anchorage of his fleet.

In the early summer of 1794 it became necessary to safeguard a number of convoys outward bound. France was known to be short of food owing to bad harvests the previous year, and would rely on imports of corn from America for at least part of her needs. In May, therefore, Howe – with a fleet so large that it resembled some of those of the seventeenth century – and seven other flag officers took charge of a complex operation in which his entire force would proceed down-Channel, and would then split up. A detachment of seven ships of the line under Rear-Admiral Montagu would protect the British 'trade'; while Howe would reconnoitre Brest in the hope of meeting the French, who, it was known, would make special efforts to bring home the ships from America. If matters went well, Howe could ensure the British merchantmen safe passage, intercept those of the French, and defeat the enemy fleet at sea. Such an outcome would indeed have been glorious, but in the event only two of the objectives, the first and the last, were attained.

The 'trade' parted from the commander-in-chief on 4 May 1794, upon which Howe steered for Ushant. The island was sighted early next day and the frigates *Phaeton* and *Latona*, covered by the *Orion* (Captain Duckworth), were ordered to look in to nearby Brest to see if the French fleet was in harbour. The captains reported that the enemy were in Brest Water. In order to tempt them out, and in the hope of meeting the grain ships, Howe sailed westward into the Atlantic. Here he cruised for a fortnight, often in misty weather. He met nothing, but in this he was unlucky. The French put to sea and at one time had been so near him that they heard his signal guns. They had also run into a British convoy, lightly escorted, and captured a number of merchantmen and the frigate *Castor*, which was commanded by Thomas Troubridge, who was later rescued by Howe.

On 19 May Howe returned to the area of Brest. Once more the *Phaeton* and *Latona* were sent scouting, covered this time by the newly built *Caesar* (Captain Molloy) and the *Leviathan* (Captain Lord Hugh Seymour). Brest Water was empty, and on retiring to report to the admiral, Lord Hugh spoke to an American skipper who said that the French fleet had sailed a few days before, the total force being about thirty-five. Howe then resumed cruising, confident that he would come across fleet or convoy, or both.

The first incident occurred two nights later, when the *Orion* made a signal for 'a strange fleet'. This proved to be merely a number of ships from the recently captured British convoy. They were promptly retaken, and the prize crews made prisoner. On 25 May two corvettes out of Brest were sighted. To everyone's astonishment, they ran straight into the British, thinking Howe's ships were their own. Howe had to burn his prizes, because he was too short-handed to spare enough officers and men to work them.

From the prisoners, it was learnt that the French were commanded by Admiral Villaret-Joyeuse, one of the few officers in the French navy still surviving after a decade on the list of captains. To keep him in order, there was a revolutionary commissar in the flagship *La Montagne*. This was Jean Bon Saint-André, a zealot for the new order. Howe's men were more impressed with the assurance shown by the prisoners than by their seamanship.

Howe also chased a French ship of the line, later discovered to be the *Audacieux*, 74 guns. This gave him confidence that he was searching the likeliest area of sea. The Frenchman got away by superior speed, and was not seen again by the British. However, early on 28 May, frigates ahead of the main body sighted the fleet of France. Howe's first object was achieved, but as Villaret-Joyeuse had the windward position, he could decline an action if he so decided.

At about 10 pm, Villaret-Joyeuse discovered Howe's distant presence and he formed line of battle; but an attack was not then his idea at all. He was in the Atlantic to guard the grain ships, and until he knew they were safe it was his duty to avoid battle. He therefore kept the wind while Howe, who was sailing in regular order in two divisions with four of the line, the *Bellerophon*, *Russell*, *Marlborough* and *Thunderer* detached as look-outs, intended to use his skill to bring about a *mêlée*.

Being far to leeward, Howe signalled instructions to harass the rear of the enemy who were on the same tack as he was. Rear-Admiral Thomas Pasley in the *Bellerophon* was in the best position to fulfil the order and his flagship, which was a seventy-four, was well supported by Seymour in the *Leviathan* and by Captain William Parker in the *Audacious*. These three ships engaged the much larger *Révolutionnaire* of 110 guns, the rear-most ship of the French fleet. By the time night had fallen, she was in a bad way. The French carried no lights during the hours of darkness, and by morning the *Révolutionnaire* had disappeared – but so had the *Audacious*, a matter over which there was some concern. The *Révolutionnaire* had actually been taken in hand by the French *Audacieux*, which had rejoined her fleet, and she succeeded in getting the three-decker safely home. The British *Audacious* had a hazardous passage back to England, but she too survived although constantly shadowed by frigates. Captain Parker later became one of St Vincent's admirals, taking part in the battle of nearly three years later in the *Prince George*.

At daylight on 29 May the French were to be seen on the bow of the British. Both fleets had become scattered, but both were soon in disciplined order. Howe's tactics were the same as before – to engage the French rear, the only portion of Villaret-Joyeuse's fleet he had any immediate hope of bringing to action. The fleets were on the same tack as on the previous evening, and although as the hours went by Howe found it possible to engage the enemy, the French ensured that this was at first at long distance. Later, however, the ships drew almost abreast of each other. Howe thereupon made the signal for his captains to tack in succession, and then to cut through the French line.

This was asking much of even the best-trained officers, and Molloy in the *Caesar*, who was leading the fleet, failed badly. On the other hand, Rear-Admiral Alan Gardner, with his flag in the three-decker *Queen*, showed splendid spirit and got so embroiled with the French that his ship received serious damage from a concentration of fire. John Hutt, the Captain, was mortally wounded and the ship was handled thereafter by the admiral himself and William Bedford, First-Lieutenant.

Other ships which pressed home their attack and earned Howe's praise were the *Royal George*, wearing the flag of Vice-Admiral Sir Alexander Hood, a successor of the ship made famous by Hawke and Kempenfelt; the *Invincible* (Captain Pakenham); and the *Bellerophon*, which was to become one of the best-known seventy-fours in the navy. She was once again to the fore under Rear-Admiral Pasley and Captain Hope. The fleet flagship herself, the *Queen Charlotte* of 100 guns, was also in close action. She lost one of her lieutenants, Roger Rawlence, who was a nephew of the Captain of the Fleet, Sir Roger Curtis.

There was soon a great deal of damage aloft in the British ships, but they gave better than they got, and it was the bad state of two Frenchman that caused Villaret-Joyeuse to run down to their help. He saved them, but at the cost of yielding the weather gauge to Howe. Henceforward, Howe would be able to bring on an action on his own terms – a chase, if the French fled; otherwise he would try to repeat the manœuvre which had already paid a reward, but which demanded steady nerves and not a little luck, that of cutting through the enemy line.

The French practice of firing high meant that much skill and activity had to be shown in the immediate repair of damage, whatever the weather conditions, if a ship was to continue to fight – and this at a time when men could be near exhaustion after battle. But the pace of sail was stately, and each ship usually had within herself the means to make her damage good without undue technical difficulty. In days of steam, the process would be called a 'self refit', which describes it accurately. Yet it could seldom take place at sea, as in the old days, because of the infinitely greater complexity of mechanical power. In the way of masts, however, a sailing ship was comparable to a modern ship dependent on a propeller, perhaps a single one. Even so, whereas a lost propeller is final, it was known for a jury rig to be attached successfully to the sorriest stumps of masts and the ship steered safely home.

Success between fleets in the time of Howe and his contemporaries depended first on superior gunnery and then on the speed at which damage could be made good. In the case of the operations of 1794 the advantage in both respects was with Howe, but a pause was necessary before a decisive encounter could be brought about. The matter was simplified by the fact that 30 May was a day of mist and light rain, during which each side could attend to its needs. Conditions were not very different the following day, when Villaret-Joyeuse had a piece of luck. He was joined by five ships of the line under Admiral Nielly. It thus so happened that, taking into account detachments of various kinds, the fleets which were to engage on 1 June were numerically nearly equal. Villaret-Joyeuse had 26 of the line present. Howe had one ship fewer. Howe's force included 7 three-decked ships, whereas Villaret-Joyeuse had only 3, but the *Montagne* (120), *Terrible* (110), and *Republicain* (110), were more heavily armed than anything in the British line. The outcome of a clash would be the result not of preponderant strength but of tactical skill on the part of the respective commanders and the resolution of individual captains.

Howe had 7 frigates, 2 fire-ships, a sloop and 2 cutters, all useful as ancillaries, but they were not expected to take part in broadside firing even when equipped for this. Howe made use of them for repeating signals, and for towing damaged vessels until the necessary repairs had been made. He also had with him a hospital ship, the *Charon*, in which was serving Thomas Trotter, Physician to the Fleet. Trotter was as enlightened a man as Sir Gilbert Blane had proved to be with Rodney in the West Indies. In health matters he looked upon Howe as a model Commander-in-Chief.

Villaret-Joyeuse, although without the amenities of such a vessel as the sadly named *Charon*, was superior in frigates, of which he had 12, in addition to which he had 8 corvettes.

At dawn on 1 June when the light wind was almost due south,

the French were about four miles north of the British. Their line was much extended, with the van on the lee beam of Howe's centre division.

At 5 am, the British bore up together so as to narrow the gap between the fleets, while keeping parallel with the enemy. It was by now apparent to Howe that Villaret-Joyeuse would not try to avoid action, and that he had as definite ideas as to the best order of battle as Howe had himself. Howe thereupon made adjustments so that the larger French ships should be suitably opposed, ensuring that the *Queen Charlotte* would engage with the *Montagne*. He ordered all his ships to fly red ensigns, so that in the confusion of fighting there would be no possibility of mistake. The French ensign at that time had tricolours in the cantons, instead of the plain white of Bourbon times; during the following year the whole ensign would become the tricolour familiar today.

It was 7 am before Howe was satisfied with his line, the *Montagne* being at that time a point or two abaft the beam of the *Queen Charlotte*. He then hove-to and passed the word for hands to go to breakfast, the enemy standing on under easy sail.

Howe's régime was more spartan than Rodney's at the time of the Saints, but his party would have included Sir Roger Curtis (the member of his retinue to whom he paid most attention, not only from the nature of his office as First Captain but through close association). Sir Andrew Douglas, the Flag or Second Captain, would also have been there. He had a much more sympathetic personality than Curtis, in the opinion of most of his fellow officers. It is possible that the ship's Chaplain, Reverend William Pace, sat down at the earl's table, scantily furnished as it would have been with most items removed to the hold, in view of impending battle.

The Chief Physician, Trotter, did not leave the *Charon* or he would possibly have been present at the meal. James Bowen, the Master of the Fleet, although a consummate seaman and navigator and a special favourite with Howe, would not, as a warrant officer, have been invited to sit down in the Great Cabin. Matters were different later, for Howe not only got Bowen promoted to quarter-deck status and shortly afterwards to post captain's rank, but caused him to be made prize agent to the fleet. Such rewards were eminently justified, and in due time Bowen attained flag rank.

In order to give his captains something to think about, Howe signalled his intention 'to pass between the ships in their lines for engaging them to leeward'. At 8.12 am he ordered the fleet 'to make sail after lying by'; and at 8.38 am the executive was hoisted

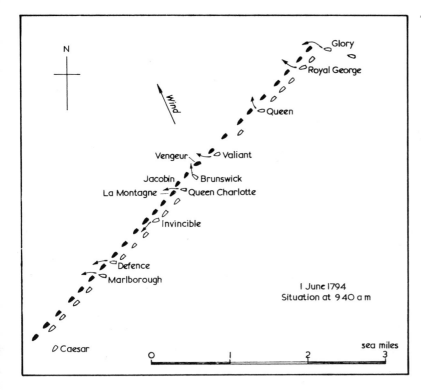

Glory

Royal George

Queen

Wind

Vengeur · Valiant

Jacobin · Brunswick

La Montagne · Queen Charlotte

Invincible

Defence

Marlborough

1 June 1794
Situation at 9.40 a.m.

Caesar

sea miles

0   1   2   3

for 'each ship independently to steer for and engage her opponent in the enemy's line'.

Howe's plan would have been clear to everyone. It was similar to that of 29 May, with the immense difference that whereas on that day great nerve and skill had been required to go through the French line when they had the advantage of the wind, now, with Villaret-Joyeuse to leeward and standing up to Howe, what was necessary was courage and a slice of luck in finding a gap. Howe prophesied that for every ship able to obey his orders to the full, a Frenchman would be taken.

The British advance, made at about 5 knots, was oblique and was therefore difficult to maintain in perfect order during the hour or so that it took to come up with the enemy. A good deal of signalling to ensure alignment was necessary both by the *Queen Charlotte* and by divisional admirals. Howe had new reason to be displeased with the *Caesar*. She still led the line, although it had become questionable whether Molloy deserved this honour. The *Caesar* did not appear to be carrying as much sail as she should, a fact noted by many captains. This was sad in Molloy who, when serving in Rodney's fleet years earlier, had not been what was known as a 'shy cock'. But the years had done him no good. This was apt to be the case, although there were remarkable exceptions – among them Howe himself.

Captain Collingwood of the *Barfleur* provided one of the best accounts of the approach in a letter to his father-in-law:

> . . . down we went under a crowd of sail, and in a manner which would have animated the coldest heart, and struck terror into the most intrepid enemy.
>
> The ship we were to engage was two ahead of the French Admiral, so that we had to go through his fire, and that of two ships next him, and received all their broadsides two or three times before we fired a gun. It was then near ten o'clock. I observed to the Admiral, that about that time our wives were going to church, but I thought the peal we should ring about the Frenchman's ears would outdo their parish bells. Lord Howe began his fire some time before we did; and he is not in the habit of firing soon.
>
> We got very near indeed, and then began such a fire as would have done you good to have heard. During the whole action the most exact order was preserved, and no accident happened but what was inevitable, and in consequence of the enemy's shot.

Collingwood was soon left on his own for he was Flag Captain to Rear-Admiral Bowyer, who fell wounded in his arms. Bowyer survived, although with the loss of a leg.

Howe said some final words on board the *Queen Charlotte* as she neared the *Montagne*. Turning to a group of officers by whom he was surrounded and shutting a little signal-book he always carried with him, he concluded, '. . . and now, gentlemen, no more book, no more signals. I look to you to do the duty of the *Queen Charlotte* in engaging the French Admiral. I do not wish the ships to be bilge and bilge, but if you lock the yard-arms so much the better, the battle will be the sooner decided.'

The duel between the commanders-in-chief did not last long because the *Montagne*, although she suffered casualties and damage from Howe's fire, was not injured aloft and she disappeared into the smoke. Observing this and fearing that Villaret-Joyeuse might make off to leeward, Howe had another thought about signalling and ordered a general chase.

This was premature, and illustrates the difficulty of exercising control of a fleet under sail once battle had been joined. Smoke and the fierceness of the fighting meant that many ships never saw the hoist. In fact, the French were not retreating – some

General engagement at the Glorious
First of June, 1794
Phillip de Loutherbourg   NMMG

could not have done so, even under orders. Seven ships, in addition
to the *Queen Charlotte*, had forced their way through the enemy
line to the leeward position and a number of prizes became certain,
since, damaged as the French ships chosen as opponents were,
they could not get away. Six duly struck their colours, and a
seventh, the *Vengeur*, was reduced to a wreck – the result of an
epic duel with Captain John Harvey of the *Brunswick*.

Harvey had stood across the French line so boldly that his
starboard anchors caught in the *Vengeur*'s fore-chains and shrouds.
After a pounding-match lasting three hours, in which the ships
were locked together and during which Harvey was mortally
wounded, the vessels at last broke apart. The *Vengeur* foundered
later, riddled with shot and dismasted, about half her crew being
rescued by British ships near at hand.

The *Brunswick*'s many casualties included Captain Saunders of
the 29th Foot (later to be known as the Worcestershire Regiment
which, with the 2nd Foot, the Queen's (Royal West Surrey)
Regiment, had detachments serving with the fleet). They were

Admiral Lord Gardner (1742–1809)
who fought the *Queen* nobly during
the course of Howe's battle
Theophilus Clarke   NPG

additional to the marines, upon whom such duties normally fell. In future, the two infantry regiments would wear a naval crown superscribed '1st June 1794' on their colours. The band of the *Brunswick* had struck up Boyce's 'Heart of Oak' as they sailed into action, and a custom developed in the 29th for this tune to be played on ceremonial occasions. Such is pride and tradition.

In a battle during the course of which most ships fought with credit (and a few magnificently), instances of valour were innumerable. Among the captains themselves, two ship's companies were looked upon as having acquitted themselves with special distinction. They were those of the *Defence*, 74 guns, and the *Queen*.

The *Defence* was commanded by Captain James Gambier who, like Richard Kempenfelt and James Saumarez, was of a religious turn. He allowed no swearing in his presence, and was familiarly known as 'Preaching Jemmy'. One of the more ribald captains hailing after the battle to congratulate as well as to commiserate with the damage suffered by his fellow-officer, called out: 'Never mind, Jemmy, the Lord loveth whom he chasteneth!'

As for the *Queen*, with her captain already a casualty and her damage from the action of three days earlier not wholly repaired, Howe would probably have excused Rear-Admiral Gardner who at the best of times was highly strung, if he had not pressed home his attack with extreme vigour. But Gardner could not have been more gallant. At the end of the battle the ship lay some distance from the rest, partially dismasted and disabled. Howe, thinking she might suffer still further from French ships as they retreated, grew concerned for her safety.

Edward Codrington, a Lieutenant belonging to the *Queen Charlotte*, later described the scene:

I went on to the poop to see Lord Howe, who was looking anxiously over the taffrail waiting for the smoke to clear away and to decide what was next to be done. He had made the signal for all ships to close round the Admiral, and seeing that the *Queen*, which had lost her mizzen mast, was a considerable way down to leeward, and in danger of being cut off by the enemy he came to the fore part of the poop under great anxiety, and called eagerly to Sir Roger Curtis, 'Go down to the *Queen*, Sir, go down to the *Queen*.' 'My Lord, we can't,' said Curtis, 'We're a mere wreck, the ship won't steer!' 'Then send everything else, Sir, directly.'

Bowen then burst out with 'She *will* steer, my Lord.' 'Try her, Sir,' said Howe. And Bowen, with a seaman's eye, watching the movement of her falling off, and getting the sprit-sail well filled to assist her, got her before the wind with her head towards the enemy.

Soon afterwards Lord Howe went to bed, tired out. For a man of sixty-eight who had had no sleep for nights and had conducted a complex engagement at the end of it all, he had done splendidly.

'On such occasions,' said Codrington, 'one is enabled familiarly to approach a man in his situation. We all got round Lord Howe, indeed, I saved him from a tumble; he was so weak that from a roll of the ship he was nearly falling into the waist. "Why, you hold me as if I were a child," he said good humouredly.'

One more scene in the fleet flagship was told to Sir John Barrow of the admiralty by one who was present.

After the battle, a deputation of petty officers and seamen requested Bowen to ask Lord Howe if they might have the gratification of congratulating his lordship on the victory he had gained, and of thanking him for having led them so gloriously.

On receiving them on the quarter-deck, Lord Howe was so affected that he could only say, with a faltering voice, and his eyes glistening with tears: 'No, no, I thank *you* – it is *you*, my brave lads, not I, that have conquered.' The honest and blunt Bowen, in telling this to a friend, said: 'I could myself have cried most heartily to see the veteran hero so affected.'

With Howe exhausted, having 'broken the line' with far more deliberation and with greater effect than Rodney, immediate

matters were left to Sir Roger Curtis. The more ardent spirits felt impatient that it should have fallen to him to exploit, or not to exploit, a decisive victory. Curtis was personally brave, and had made his name years earlier as one of General Eliott's pillars of strength during the great siege of Gibraltar, being knighted for his services at that time. But, as with Molloy of the *Caesar*, time had done him no good. He was fussy and capricious, a strange choice as chief of staff for such a man as Howe. Sir Andrew Douglas might have urged that a detachment of the least-damaged ships should be sent off in pursuit of the French, but Douglas had been wounded in the head. Although he remained on duty, he never fully recovered.

Curtis kept the signal for closing round the *Queen Charlotte* flying, and the fleet repaired damages during the evening and night which followed the battle, also most of the next day. The *Queen* astonished everyone by her exertions. This left the French to make their way home unharassed, although one or two of their ships were in tow. Howe made no such remark next day such as that of Rodney to Hood after the Saints, when he said he thought they had done very well as it was but he could be reasonably satisfied. Six French ships would make a fine show at Spithead, and he had lost none of his own fleet. On the other hand, owing to the stubbornness of French resistance, his casualties had not been light. They were to include one other captain besides Hutt of the *Queen* and Harvey of the *Brunswick*: this was James Montagu, commanding a ship of the same name.

As for the French convoy from America, Howe knew from Villaret-Joyeuse's behaviour in standing up to attack that it must be nearing France. His own ships could not hope to intercept it but he had hopes that Rear-Admiral Montagu, after seeing the British 'trade' into safe latitudes, would come upon the grain ships, which would have no very strong escort in view of the fact that the main French strength was with Villaret-Joyeuse. Montagu had orders to search for it, but had no luck.

The battle had taken place some 429 miles into the Atlantic, more or less in the latitude of Ushant, and it was ten days before the French fleet anchored in Bertheaume Roads, just outside Brest. Saint-André was disinclined to face the reception that he and the admiral might have expected for returning with a depleted and battered fleet. The very next day, however, the convoy of 116 sail was sighted, after a two-months passage from Chesapeake Bay and not having been seen by a single British vessel. With this drastic turn for the better, all forebodings could be forgotten in a triumphant entry into port. A legend was now generated that the *Vengeur* had sunk with all hands, a sad libel on British sailors who had saved so many of her crew.

When the king had news of the action from Curtis, who went home in a fast ship with Howe's despatches, he referred to the event as 'glorious'. But the king was a realist and when fuller information was available, including word from Rear-Admiral Montagu, he added: 'one cannot help being mortified that probably the great convoy from America will arrive safe in France'. In sum, Howe's cruise had been a tactical success, but a strategic disappointment.

Mortified as he might be in one particular, George III was so delighted that his fleet soon after the start of another war had been so well conducted and had fought so stoutly, that he announced his intention of going to Portsmouth, accompanied by the queen, to congratulate Howe and to present him with a sword embellished with diamonds. The fountain of honour would gush, though the fall of its spray would be eccentric. The king had promised Howe the Garter, but Pitt, the Prime Minister, begged

Obverse of gold medal awarded to
commanders at the Glorious First of
June, 1794   NMMG

that this should be bestowed, for political reasons, on the Duke
of Portland and that the admiral should be offered a marquisate
instead. The king agreed with great reluctance. Howe said he
would have the Garter or nothing, but for the moment he had
to be content with the sword and a gold medal and chain. He
got his blue riband in due course, though not for another three
years. When it came, it was the only Garter ever given for services
purely naval in character.

In the past it had been customary to reward successful naval
and military commanders with knighthoods, baronetcies and
peerages, according to circumstances. This practice was continued,
but the king also established a procedure for the award of gold
chains and medals to flag officers in particular cases, and gold
medals of a smaller size to captains of ships of the line.

The rewards after the First of June were more liberal than after the Saints, but that event had occurred in a time of political turmoil and depression. Thomas Graves, the admiral who had been in command at the Chesapeake and who had been Howe's second, received an Irish barony; so did Alexander Hood, just as his brother, Samuel, had been favoured after Rodney's victory. Rear-Admirals Bowyer, Gardner and Pasley were made baronets, as was Curtis. Unhappily, there was one Admiral, Benjamin Caldwell, and eight captains who were omitted from the distribution altogether.

The exceptions, as anyone concerned with awards should have known, were not only mortified, as were their ship's companies, but they were bitter and sometimes heartbroken. Caldwell had been fifth in order of seniority, senior to Gardner and Pasley, and he never forgave the slight: nor, among the captains, could Collingwood, whose admiral was among those favoured. Collingwood felt so indignant, as did fellow captains on his behalf, that three years later, after the battle of St Vincent, when there was a distribution of medals to admirals and captains without exception, he refused to receive his until the wrong had been righted. On the representation of his new commander-in-chief he was sent medals for both actions by Lord Spencer, then at the head of the admiralty.

Collingwood and others blamed Curtis's partiality for the distinctions that were drawn, and this was probably correct. If so the necessary deductions were made, and trouble of this sort never occurred again in quite the same way. As for Molloy, feeling against him was such that he requested a court-martial, a course which Howe did not favour. Molloy got his way, though the court was not convened for nearly a year. The verdict was that although he was acquitted of cowardice, he was convicted of not having done his best to pass through the French line on 29 May and for not taking a proper station when coming into action on 1 June. He was dismissed his ship, and not employed again.

The king's visit to Portsmouth was a grand affair, and generated great enthusiasm and loyalty. It was marred only by the disappointment of the undecorated. In London and in the country generally there was great rejoicing. In answer to demand, many artists set to work to produce versions of the action, spurred on by the earlier success of Benjamin West's picture of the 'Death of Wolfe', which remained a best-seller in the field of prints.

Mather Brown in particular made a poster-like version of a scene on the deck of the *Queen Charlotte* (the planks running the wrong way), in which Howe, Curtis, Douglas and others were represented in meticulous detail. The central incident showed the death in action of Lieutenant John Neville of the Queen's Regiment. He was seen collapsed and in the arms of Walter Lock, Third Lieutenant of the ship, attended by Ensign James Tudor.

Although the picture was greatly liked at the time, has been admired ever since, and is often reproduced, it provides a good example of how little battle pictures resemble the real thing. The impeccable and spotless uniforms shown so well by the artist were at the time stowed below where they would not be stained by powder and the bloody ingredients of action. A forbear of the present writer, who took passage in a West Indiaman not long after the battle, found a seaman on board who had served in the *Queen Charlotte*. He said that during the fighting Howe put on an old fur hat, and that afterwards he looked as grimy as any tramp.

9 Copenhagen Twice Assaulted

So far from declining in importance after the troubles which had led to the Battle of the Sound in the seventeenth century, the Scandinavian countries, and those which controlled the eastern shores of the Baltic, continued to be a source of anxiety to Britain in time of war. Although interruption to the flow of their resources was the main reason, there were others. They were the outlet for an expanding trade; and their navies, although not of the first rank, could be a useful supplement in any coalition.

Serious trouble had arisen at the time of the War of American Independence, when a combination of northern powers, Denmark, Sweden and Russia, all of which were profiting from the needs of countries at war, established what became known as armed neutrality. The leading principles agreed upon by the participants were that neutrals should be free to engage in the coastal and colonial trades of belligerents; that enemy property carried in neutral shipping should not be subject to seizure; that ships under convoy of a man-of-war should not be liable to search; that naval stores should be excluded from the category of contraband; and that a blockade, to be respected, must be efficient.

No such principles could be accepted by any power engaged in a maritime war. They were resisted, with limited success but consistent firmness. When Britain became involved in a conflict of still greater scope, this time with the France of Napoleon, the idea of an armed neutrality was revived by Tsar Paul I of Russia, the original neutrality being enlarged by the addition of Prussia. Over and above the danger threatened by this move, there was a fear that the fleets of the northern powers might be employed directly in the French service. To take precautions against such a possibility was natural enough. It led to drastic preventative action, of so bold a kind that it could not hope to have met with universal approval.

Early in 1801, negotiations having failed, and the Tsar having arbitrarily seized British shipping in Russian ports, a fleet was assembled with the idea of overawing the northern powers, by force of arms if necessary. At that time, St Vincent was 1st Lord of the Admiralty. He had been appointed by Henry Addington, who succeeded the younger Pitt in a government which was described by some as being 'of No Talents'. The popular judgement was too harsh, although, as a popular jingle put it:

> Pitt is to Addington
> As London is to Paddington

St Vincent was undoubtedly behind the idea of using naval power to counter a threat essentially maritime. Where his judgement was at fault was in his choice of commanders. The officer chosen to lead the sortie was Sir Hyde Parker, the second son of that crusty character 'Vinegar' Parker who had been much at variance with Rodney. The chief reason was that Parker happened to be available. He had served earlier in the Mediterranean, where he had not made a good impression on captains such as Collingwood and Nelson. He was sixty-two, and by nature indolent. He was rich, and had recently married a plump young woman known to the irreverent as 'batter pudding'.

The 1st Lord chose Nelson as second in command. Although Nelson was in some ways not averse to returning to active service, he had been long in the Mediterranean and would have preferred less chilly parts than the Baltic. His personal affairs were in so critical a state that anyone who knew him well must have had doubts how he would sustain campaigning. Parker, although senior to Nelson, had a fighting record in no way comparable. He would certainly need stimulus from the younger man if the expedition was not to end in disaster or humiliation, or both.

Pressure had to be applied even before the fleet weighed from Great Yarmouth. Parker had arranged a ball, and Nelson had to remind him (via friends on the Board of Admiralty) that he was ordered north on urgent business and must not dally. For his own part, Nelson wished the affair over and done with as soon as possible. His marriage was now in ruins, and his war wounds were playing him up. Emma Hamilton, his mistress, had recently given birth to his child, Horatio. This gave Nelson, hitherto a childless man, the greatest pleasure. He could scarcely wait before paying the infant more attention than the glimpse he had snatched during a flying visit to London.

Although Parker was hustled off, before he sailed he made no attempt to take Nelson into his confidence. Indeed, it was not until the fleet was approaching the operational area that Parker

seems to have realised the complexities of the task before him. By that time it was virtually certain that Denmark, first on the list for intimidation, would resist. Russia, the mainstay of the armed neutrality, would, of course, be actively hostile. Only the attitude of Sweden was uncertain. King Gustavus IV Adolphus was known to look upon Napoleon as the Beast of the Apocalypse, but the general view was that he had a screw loose and might not have his country behind him.

Parker took the fleet to within a few miles of Elsinore, anchoring while he decided what next to do. The lack of preliminary planning was such that, even at this stage, the commander-in-chief was not certain whether to approach Copenhagen by way of the Sound or the Belts, the latter being more difficult to navigate and a far longer though less well-guarded route. Nelson thought the choice mattered less than speed. 'I am of opinion,' he wrote to Parker on 24 March, 'the boldest measures are the safest; and our Country demands a most vigorous exertion of her force, directed

The British fleet passing the fortress of Kronborg, 1801   *Robert Dodd* NMMG

with judgement. In supporting you, my dear Sir Hyde, through the arduous and important task you have undertaken, no exertion of head or heart shall be wanted from your most obedient and faithful servant *Nelson and Brontë*.'

Nelson would have favoured by-passing Copenhagen, leaving a small squadron of observation, and proceeding at once to beard the Russians who were the main source of trouble. This shrewd plan would, if followed, have saved many lives, but Parker was not convinced of its soundness. Dithering as usual, he next enquired of the governor of Kronborg Castle, guarding the Sound, whether he would challenge the passage of the British fleet. The answer came in no uncertain terms: he would. The commander-in-chief then consulted Nelson, Captain Murray of the *Edgar*, who knew the Baltic well, and his Flag Captain, Otway. All of them favoured risking the Sound, and Parker agreed.

On 30 March, the day the fleet weighed, the guns mounted at Kronborg thundered, but wasted their shot. Parker kept his ships near the Swedish shore, where the batteries, significantly, were silent. The British came safely to anchor between the island of Hven, once famed for the observatory of the astronomer Tycho Brahe, and the larger Amager, on which part of Copenhagen was built. A series of detailed reconnaissances then began in which Parker himself took part, use being made of the frigate *Amazon* (Captain Riou), the smartest in the fleet.

Before the final stages of the operation, Parker summoned a regular council of war. This was in accordance with regular naval procedure, but Nelson detested the practice. He held the view that 'if a man consults whether he is to fight, when he has the power in his own hands, *it is certain his opinion is against fighting*'. As he plainly foresaw that fighting would be necessary, he made it his business to stimulate the council as to convince them that any other course would be stupid. The result was that Parker gave him a free hand for the conduct of the attack on the moored ships and the forts which guarded the approaches to the harbour and dockyard of the Danish capital. Parker himself, with the larger ships, would cruise in the offing, ready to prevent any sortie by a sea-going squadron. It was as good a plan as could have been contrived, and Nelson spent the night of 1 April dictating orders in his cabin. He had already infected the captains under his immediate command with his own energy and fire. His circle also included Lieutenant-Colonel the Hon William Stewart of the Rifle Brigade, senior officer of the troops on board the *Elephant*, 74 guns, to which Nelson had transferred his flag. Stewart very soon came under Nelson's spell, and recorded as many anecdotes about him as did Colonel Drinkwater after the battle of St Vincent.

In addition to the moored ships and the land defences, nature herself made the approaches to Copenhagen formidable. A series of protective banks and shoals included what was known as the Middle Ground, off which was a channel called the King's Deep which Nelson would have to negotiate in order to bombard the Danes.

Uncertain factors were wind and pilotage. The fleet had been favoured with a northerly wind to enable it to reach Copenhagen speedily, to the south of which Parker anchored. It would need to change direction almost completely in order to favour successful negotiation of the King's Deep. Those experienced in Baltic weather were optimistic in this matter, and they proved to be right. Pilotage was more worrying. Few sailing masters in Parker's fleet knew anything about local conditions, and of those who professed knowledge most proved wrong. Indeed, when the

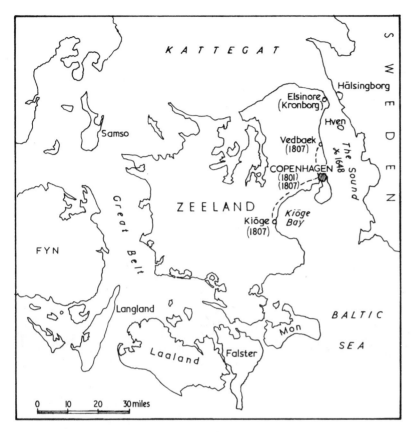

wind duly changed, on 2 April, many captains conned their ships themselves – notably in the case of William Bligh of the *Glatton*, the same officer who had been with Captain Cook and against whom the crew of the *Bounty* had mutinied.

Of the twelve ships of the line at Nelson's disposal, three ran aground during the approach, reducing his effective force by a quarter even before action began. Two of these, the *Bellona* and the *Russell*, were to play at least a distant part. The third, which happened to be Nelson's beloved old command the *Agamemnon*, failed to round the Middle Ground at all. To his chagrin, her Captain, Robert Fancourt, became a mere spectator.

Shortly after 10 am there began one of the fiercest cannonades Nelson had ever experienced. The Danes, moored as they were, could not withdraw. They could only fight or surrender. They were defending their beloved city; they were under the eye of their prince royal, the effective ruler of the kingdom, and they had the resources of a dockyard behind them. Their resistance was stout and sustained and the British frigates particularly, which were at the head of Nelson's line forming a signal link with

Nelson's attack on Copenhagen, 1801
Robert Dodd   NMMG

Parker, were suffering badly from the guns of the Trekroner battery, to which they could make no adequate reply.

At 1.30 pm, when action had continued for some three hours and Danish fire seemed to have begun to slacken, Parker, fretting at Nelson's prolonged ordeal, made a signal for him to disengage. This was not, as Southey tried to make out in his famous *Life*, permissive. It was peremptory and it was utterly misguided. Nelson's ships were in a most dangerous position, both navigationally and from enemy fire. He knew what he was doing and how close he was to success. On being told of the order from the commander-in-chief, his reaction was noted by Colonel Stewart who was standing near him. It is one of the most famous incidents in the annals or war.

> [Nelson] continued his walk, and did not appear to take notice of the signal. The Lieutenant, meeting his Lordship at the next turn, asked 'whether he should repeat it?' Lord Nelson answered, 'No, acknowledge it.' On the officer returning to the poop, his Lordship called after him, 'Is No. 16 [for close action] still hoisted?' The Lieutenant answering in the affirmative, Lord Nelson said: 'Mind you keep it so.'

He now walked the deck considerably agitated, which was

always known by his moving the stump of his right arm. After a turn or two, he said to me in a quick manner: 'Do you know what's shown on board of the Commander-in-Chief – No. 39.' On asking him what that meant, he answered: 'Why, to leave off action!' 'Leave off action!' he repeated, and then added, with a shrug, 'Now, damn me if I do.' He also observed, I believe to Captain Foley: 'You know, Foley, I have only one eye. I have a right to be blind sometimes,' and then, with an archness peculiar to his character, putting his glass to his blind eye, he exclaimed: 'I really do not see the Signal!'

Nelson's second in command, together with all the ships of the line in his immediate charge, continued action as if Parker had never intervened. It was a different story with the frigates, which were nearer the fleet flagship. They obeyed, and tragedy resulted. As he altered course, Captain Riou of the *Amazon* was killed by a shot from the Trekroner. Parker had become responsible for the death of one of the best officers in the navy.

Firing, heavy or intermittent, continued for some hours after the signal, but gradually most of the Danish ships and hulks were either wrecked, burnt, badly damaged, or had surrendered. But the forts kept up their steady and accurate fire, and it was this which determined Nelson to send a note ashore under a flag of truce. He wrote

Lord Nelson has directions to spare Denmark, when no longer resisting but if the firing is continued on the part of Denmark, Lord Nelson will be obliged to set on fire all the floating batteries he has taken, without having the power of saving the Brave Danes who have defended them.

> Dated on board His Britannick Majesty's Ship *Elephant*
> Copenhagen Roads April 2nd 1801
> *Nelson and Brontë, Vice Admiral under the Command of Admiral Sir Hyde Parker.*

To the Brothers of Englishmen
The Danes.

The original, preserved in Denmark, is said to have been written on the casing of the *Elephant*'s rudder-head. Obviously Nelson ordered the ship's guns to cease fire, or he could not have written steadily. Wallis, the purser, copied the note for the letter-book. His version does not always strictly follow the original, though the purport is the same. The missive was carefully sealed with wax and sent ashore.

British Tars towing the Danish Fleet into Harbour; — the Broadbottom Leviathan trying to swamp Billy's old Boat, & the little Corsican tottering on the Clouds of Ambition.

The Danish fleet being brought to
England as the result of the
Copenhagen expedition
Cartoon of 1807 by *Gillray*
British Museum

A little after 3 pm the Danish Adjutant-General, Lindholm, reached the *Elephant* with an enquiry from the Danish prince royal as to the exact purpose of the message, but meanwhile fire ceased. Captain Thomas Fremantle of the *Ganges*, a close friend of Nelson, noted that the pause 'was certainly as convenient for *us* as for the Enemy, as we had several ships on shore and most of the ships engaged crippled so completely that it was with difficulty they could sail out'. Casualties on both sides had been very heavy, 253 British killed and at least 790 Danes, with many others wounded.

Not the least extraordinary part of Parker's conduct was that having allowed Nelson to shoulder all the burden and hazard of fighting the battle, he then put upon him the conduct of the negotiations which followed. Nelson must have wondered what Parker was in the Baltic for. However, in a long interview with the prince royal, he gained the points he was sent ashore to establish: that the fleet could provision in Denmark and that an armistice would continue.

Colonel Stewart was sent to England at the same time as

Parker's despatches in which, although the commander-in-chief paid generous tribute to Nelson (he could scarcely have done otherwise), he omitted mention of his signal and did not stress the fact that as a result of the vacancies caused by battle casualties he had promoted his own favourites, not those who deserved honour from their conduct in the fighting. He was within his rights, but soreness was felt long after the campaign ended.

Stewart, being a Nelson partisan as well as an eye-witness, could tell the full story. St Vincent was duly impressed. Not only did he supersede Parker at once, but he appointed Nelson in his place. A little later, when Nelson's health led him to beg the 1st Lord to relieve him, St Vincent wrote:

> ... to find a fit successor, your Lordship knows, is no easy task, for I never saw a man in our profession, excepting yourself and Troubridge, who possessed the magic art of infusing the same spirit into others which inspired his own actions, exclusive of other talents and habits of business not common to naval officers.

Parker felt himself ill-used, and he would have started a pamphlet war on his own behalf had he not been persuaded by the friendly advice of Nelson that it would do him more harm than good. What grieved Nelson was that while he himself was given a step in the peerage, his captains got no official recognition. The reasons for this were various. Among them was the fact that the country was not officially at war with Denmark at the time of the attack.

Since St Vincent would deny Nelson nothing, he was allowed to sail home a few weeks after the battle and was thus able to enjoy one of the rare summers he spent in England. The admiralty even found a 'fit successor'. This was Sir Charles Morice Pole, a special favourite with Nelson, who had known him since boyhood, and thought the world of him. Pole had only a few weeks in the Baltic before the command was dissolved. He made good use of his time by investigating the navigational problems of the Great Belt in his flagship the *St George*. His observations were of value when, a few years later, the Belt became the route used by British convoys to and from the Baltic.

By one of those ironies which occur so often in the melancholy history of warfare, the assault on Copenhagen proved to have been unnecessary. Tsar Paul I had been murdered by his entourage a week before the battle, but the news did not reach Denmark until too late. Paul's successor, Alexander I, reversed Russian policy in respect of the armed neutrality, and released the British ships held in Russian ports. When Captain Fremantle was sent to St Petersburg as a British emissary, he received courteous treatment and remarked that from all he heard about Tsar Paul, he wondered he had survived so long.

Before he left the Baltic, Nelson stated that sooner or later there would be renewed trouble with Denmark, a proud country which had been outraged by the action of the British fleet. He proved himself a prophet.

The sequel came six years later, when Nelson himself was dead. After tergiversations of policy which marked his whole life as sovereign ruler, Alexander I agreed at Tilsit, in a treaty signed with Napoleon on 7 July 1807, that he would make common cause with France in enforcing the commercial, political and military exclusion of Britain from the continent. The tsar would be responsible for the Baltic area. This implied that he would coerce Denmark and Sweden into closing their ports to the British flag.

It happened that George Canning succeeded to the office of foreign secretary in March 1807. Canning had been a great admirer of Nelson. At the time of Trafalgar he had been treasurer of the navy, and had dined with Nelson on board the *Victory* the very day the admiral sailed to join the fleet for the last time. And now, as history seemed to be repeating itself in a sinister way, the foreign secretary, in close and secret collaboration with the admiralty, then headed by Henry Phipps, planned a sudden seizure of the Danish fleet which would result, or so he hoped, in the terrorisation of the northern powers.

The *coup de main* was successful, although in a longer-term view policy misfired. It alienated the Danes entirely and angered the Russians, without doing anything to remove the impression on the continent that Britain had not the means, and possibly not the will, to support effectively any state which resisted the power of France. Wellington's peninsular campaigns were in the future. So far little had occurred to encourage any belief in Britain as a land power, whatever might be her capabilities at sea.

Admiral James Gambier who, as a post captain, had fought the *Defence* so well at the Glorious First of June, was put in charge of a considerable fleet. Lord Cathcart was given command of an army which included Sir Arthur Wellesley among its senior officers. Although he had had a brilliant career already as a soldier in

India, he was not trusted by the Whitehall pundits in a European command without a 'nurse' in the shape of General Robert Stewart.

This time everything was well planned and the Danes, who knew that a French army of 70,000 men was encamped near their border, were to be faced with what Canning called 'a balance of opposite dangers'. Copenhagen was by now invulnerable to direct attack from seaward, so landings would have to be made under cover of the fleet.

The main body anchored near Elsinore, and a squadron of four of the line and three frigates under Commodore Richard Keats was sent through the Belts to secure the other entrance to the Baltic. The result was that no considerable reinforcement could be brought from the Jutland mainland to Zealand, on which island most of Copenhagen stands. The speed and secrecy of dispositions was the decisive factor in the brief campaign which followed. Zealand being isolated, and the bulk of the Danish army being in Holstein, the troops were likely to be opposed only by militia.

A landing was made on 15 August 1807 at Vedbaek, between Elsinore and Copenhagen. Six days later other forces landed south of the capital, and a pincer movement began. Copenhagen was duly invested, bombarded, and set on fire. It fell on 5 September because the veteran commander, General Payman, considered that serious fires which had been caused in the timberyards would otherwise destroy the city.

Wellesley showed an example of his skill in dealing with the only serious attempt at relief. He had the Danes winkled out of entrenched positions near Kiöge at the cost of 172 casualties. 'We are very unpopular in the country', he wrote home, admitting sadly that although his men fought well they were all too apt to pillage. The future Duke of Wellington's most lasting memorial of the affair was his famous chestnut horse, Copenhagen. This creature was born to a fellow officer's mare shortly after the fighting ended.

The British commanders, who reaped a princely harvest in the way of prize-money – about £300,000 between them – insisted on the surrender of the Danish fleet as an essential to any accommodation. They also arranged that the citadel and dockyard should be occupied for six weeks, and that the garrison would be withdrawn as soon as the object of the sortie had been achieved. The operation showed how serious the threat might have been had Napoleon been able to employ the Danish fleet in his own service. The numbers of ships of the line taken back to England totalled 15, 6 more being destroyed as useless or incomplete; 15 frigates were also removed, and over 30 smaller vessels. And on the day that the immediate fate of Copenhagen was decided, the frigate *Quebec*, supported by the *Majestic* of 74 guns, took the North Sea island of Heligoland from Denmark. The value of this capture was as an *entrepôt*, such as Malta was proving to be in the Mediterranean.

It was the beginning of a series of events of ever-increasing complexity in the Baltic, the constant factor being the continued adherence of Denmark to the cause of France. Each summer from 1808 until 1812, when Napoleon made his disastrous advance into Russia, a British fleet under Sir James Saumarez, with his flag in the *Victory*, dominated the Baltic. He and his advisers arranged a system of trading in which false papers and identities played a prominent part. Supplies continued to reach Britain in spite of anything Napoleon could do.

Although there were no full-scale battles, there was much fighting in defence of convoys, Danish light craft playing a gallant part in attack, chiefly by night. Because of stormy weather, there were also tragic marine losses, including that of the three-decker *St George* and other veteran ships of the line.

Sweden, whose statesmen never forgave Gustavus IV for the loss of Finland to Russia (which was one of the greater events of the period), expelled him from the country, importing the French Marshal Bernadotte as heir to the throne of the Vasas.

At the general settlement after the long war ended in 1815, Sweden took Norway from Denmark as compensation for the loss of Finland. The union was never popular. It lasted for less than a century, after which Norway's medieval autonomy was restored under a Danish-born king.

The losers were the Danes, who paid grievously for their loyalty to France. Perhaps they are right to emphasise other phases of their history than one which brought them so much undeserved suffering, and two separate assaults on Copenhagen.

10 HMS *Lion* at Jutland

Denmark managed to preserve her neutrality during the first of the two great wars of the present century, though the only major fleet action which occurred between 1914 and 1918 took place not far from her coast. The British called it the Battle of Jutland. The Germans named it, perhaps more logically, after the Skagerrak, the expanse of often-turbulent water which separates Denmark from Norway.

It was on 31 May 1916 that the British Grand Fleet and the German High Seas Fleet met in battle. When the last casualty had been inflicted, during the early hours of 1 June, 14 British and 11 German ships had been sunk; 6,097 British and 2,551 German sailors had died, and Jellicoe, the British Commander-in-Chief, was in possession of the battle area, his main force intact. In terms of proportion of loss it was a notable German success, particularly as Scheer, the German Commander-in-Chief, was greatly out-numbered. Strategically, the British retained over-all control of the surface of the sea, which they had held from the outbreak of war nearly two years earlier. They could send ships and men where they wanted, anywhere in the world. The Germans could not.

The heavy British loss in capital ships, the battle-cruisers *Queen Mary*, *Indefatigable* and *Invincible*, occurred during the earlier part of the engagement. The result was due to good gunnery by the Germans and to poor protection against flash, which caused all three ships to blow up with only a handful of survivors. What is not often realised is that it was due to the order of an officer of the Royal Marines, and action taken upon that order, that a severe initial setback did not become a full-scale disaster for the British.

Scheer's hope was to entice the British battle-cruiser force led by Vice-Admiral Sir David Beatty into an engagement with his own battle-cruisers led by Admiral Franz von Hipper. Scheer thus hoped to fall upon the British in overwhelming strength, von Hipper being the bait he knew would attract Beatty. The first contact between scouting cruisers was made at 2.30 pm on a

Admiral Lord Beatty (1871–1936)
who commanded the British battle-
cruisers at Jutland, 1916   *Sir*
William Orpen   Scottish National
Portrait Gallery

Admiral Franz von Hipper (1863–
1932) who commanded the German
battle-cruisers at Jutland
photo: Imperial War Museum   IWM

day of varying visibility off the west coast of Denmark. The battle-cruisers came into action at 3.48 pm, the Germans having considerable advantage of the light, of which they made good use.

von Hipper's duty was to draw Beatty towards Scheer's main fleet, which was well out of sight to the south of him but coming up fast. Beatty had 6 battle-cruisers to von Hipper's 5. Beatty had, moreover, the support of 4 new and fast battleships under the command of Rear-Admiral Hugh Evan-Thomas. He was in superior force and he naturally accepted battle at once, having complete confidence in his ships and men. They had proved themselves in action before, and if he waited for Evan-Thomas to close up from a distance of about 10 miles in his rear he might miss the chance of destroying von Hipper, who certainly could not be expected to wait for an enemy reinforcement!

Within forty minutes of the opening broadsides, Beatty had lost two of his great ships. Each of them was firing well at the time, but each was highly vulnerable to plunging shell. The *Indefatigable* went up in smoke and flame with a thunderous roar at 4.05 pm, and the *Queen Mary* just over twenty minutes later. Beatty's remark to Flag Captain Chatfield as he saw the gaps in

HMS *Queen Mary* blown up at Jutland   *photo: Imperial War Museum*   IWM

Jutland, 31 May 1916 – the battle-cruiser stage, 3.25 to 6.15 pm

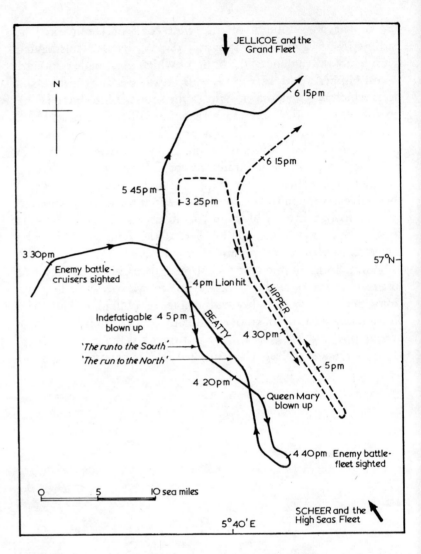

his line has passed into legend: 'There seems to be something wrong with our bloody ships today.'

What was not then known to the admiral was that he was lucky to be alive to make any comment at all. At about 4 pm an 11-inch German shell made a direct hit on Q gun turret of the *Lion*, his flagship. This turret was amidships, and the shell put both turret guns out of action and killed nearly a hundred officers and men. That the *Lion* herself did not go the way of the *Indefatigable* and the *Queen Mary* was because of the presence of mind of Major F. J. W. Harvey of the Royal Marines. Although terribly burnt and with only moments to live, he gave the order to close the magazine doors and flood the magazines, which were far below in the depths of the ship. Some of those who carried out

HMS *Lion*, Beatty's flagship at
Jutland. Q turret, amidships, was
put out of action early in the battle
photo: Imperial War Museum IWM

his orders were later found dead with their hands on the door
clips. In his account of the battle, Winston Churchill remarked:
'In the long, rough history of the Royal Marines there is no name
and no deed which in its character and consequences ranks above
this.' This was the exact truth. Major Harvey was posthumously
awarded the Victoria Cross, and the value of his action is beyond
calculation.

Such is the difficulty of demolishing legend that the senior
surviving officer of marines serving in the *Lion*, Captain (later
Lieutenant-Colonel) F. R. Jones, who had the sad duty of identi-
fying the dead from Q turret by the dim light of a torch, spent
many years trying to correct the statement, which even now
occurs in accounts of the battle, that Major Harvey's legs were

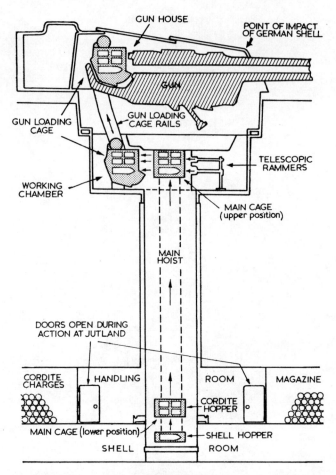

GUN HOUSE

POINT OF IMPACT
OF GERMAN SHELL

GUN LOADING
CAGE

GUN LOADING
CAGE RAILS

GUN

TELESCOPIC
RAMMERS

WORKING
CHAMBER

MAIN CAGE
(upper position)

MAIN
HOIST

DOORS OPEN DURING
ACTION AT JUTLAND

CORDITE
CHARGES

HANDLING

ROOM

MAGAZINE

CORDITE
HOPPER

MAIN CAGE (lower position)

SHELL HOPPER
ROOM

SHELL

blown off when the turret was hit. Had this been so, he could not
have reached the voice-pipe to give the vital order. Harvey was
terribly burnt, but he was not dismembered. He had served in the
Lion in two earlier actions, at Heligoland Bight in August 1914
and off the Dogger Bank in January 1916. In the second affair, the
Germans concentrated fire on Beatty's flagship, damaged her
engines and forced her out of the line. Lacking his presence during
critical moments, the enemy were not pursued and the sole result
of the engagement was the sinking of the *Blücher*, the weakest ship
in Hipper's force, after a magnificent defence. It was realised, as a
result of battle damage, that capital ships of the High Seas Fleet
needed more efficient protection against flash. The necessary
steps were taken, which was not the case in the British fleet.

From his earlier experiences, Major Harvey knew that the *Lion*
would be the target for heavy fire, and had thought out the
necessary steps to take if an emergency arose. The shell which did
the damage hit Q turret at the junction of the front roof plates,

which it penetrated, bursting in the gun house. When a sergeant of marines, hatless and blood-stained, went to report to the captain of the ship, one of the lieutenants looked over the side of the bridge and saw that the armoured roof of the turret 'had been folded back like an open sardine tin. Thick yellow smoke was rolling up in clouds from the gaping hole, and the guns were cocked in the air.' As he remarked, it was astonishing that 'all this should have happened within a few yards of where Beatty was standing, and that none of us on the bridge should have heard the detonation'. Such is the din of battle.

A second explosion followed shortly after the first, when smouldering material fell on a full charge of cordite in the loading cage below the turret. The cordite exploded, the flash igniting a charge in the hopper used for sending shell up the hoist to the guns. But by then the magazine doors were closed, the turret's magazine was flooding, and the *Lion* was saved from instant destruction.

By an extraordinary chance, an almost exactly similar incident had taken place on board the cruiser *Kent*, when on 8 December 1914, she had been in pursuit of the German cruiser *Nürnberg* at the Battle of the Falkland Islands. A shell struck a gun casement and ignited a charge, the flash going down the hoist as in the *Lion*. Sergeant Charles Mayes of the marines was stationed at the bottom of the hoist and, on his own initiative, immediately flooded the ammunition compartment, an action which, in the opinion of the captain, saved the ship. Mayes survived to receive the Conspicuous Gallantry medal.

If, at Jutland, the *Lion* had blown up, coherent leadership in the battle-cruiser force would have been lost, temporarily at least, despite the skill and spirit of the subordinate flag officers, Rear Admirals Brock and Pakenham. The three remaining battle-cruisers, two of them already damaged, would almost certainly have been eliminated. Not long after the knocking out of Q turret, the *Lion* herself had one further escape. A signal boy saw a large unexploded German shell lying close to a fire burning fiercely near the fore funnel. A party rolled it over the side.

When Evan-Thomas's battleships came fully into action at about 4.20 pm it was the turn of the Germans to suffer. 'Nothing but the poor quality of the British bursting charges saved us from disaster', von Hipper recorded. And when at 4.38 pm the vigilant Rear-Admiral Goodenough reported sighting the main German fleet from the cruiser *Southampton*, Beatty was able to alter course northward and lead Scheer towards Jellicoe, after confirming the presence of the High Seas Fleet with his own eyes. Scheer had no knowledge that the British Grand Fleet was even at sea, let alone approaching at high speed. Intelligence, which did not always serve Jellicoe well, had in this instance alerted him to be in the right area at the right time.

By pressing across the German line of advance, Beatty was able to prevent von Hipper and Scheer from sighting the British commander-in-chief until – to his astonishment and consternation – Scheer was confronted with 'the belching guns of an interminable line of heavy ships extending from north-west to north-east'.

The first capital ships from Jellicoe's fleet to engage the enemy were a group of three battle-cruisers led by Rear-Admiral Horace Hood. Observers agree that the shooting of the *Invincible*, which flew Hood's flag, was splendid, but at 6.30 pm exactly the same fate overtook her as had come so suddenly upon the *Indefatigable* and the *Queen Mary*. The tragedy proved beyond all question the vulnerability of the battle-cruisers. It was indeed merciful for Beatty that Hood's squadron, which in normal circumstances would have been with him, had been ordered to Scapa Flow for gunnery practice with the Grand Fleet, Evan-Thomas being sent to Beatty as a replacement. No reinforcement available at the time was stronger, faster or better-trained, and it may be said that Evan-Thomas's battleships, the *Barham*, *Warspite*, *Malaya* and *Valiant*, did more than their share in redressing the adverse result of the run to the south.

When battle was fully joined, victory eluded Jellicoe. Twice, at 6.40 pm and again at 7.18 pm, when Scheer appeared to be trapped, he executed an extraordinary manœuvre, difficult in the extreme and requiring an exceptional standard of competence. He reversed the course of his big ships simultaneously. This was known to the Germans as the 'Battle Turn About' – their term was *Gefechtskehrtwendung*. Jellicoe would not have considered the order practical, or ever likely to be necessary, but it was successfully carried out by his opponent. Later on, darkness became Scheer's friend, and during the course of the short summer night he was able to force his way through the British covering screens of cruisers and destroyers to the safety of harbour. It was not a glorious retreat. Two big ships, the old battleship *Pommern* and the battle-cruiser *Lutzow* were sunk, but by any standard it was a highly creditable one.

Two traps had been sprung, and had failed, during that tumultouus smoke-filled day in the North Sea. Beatty and his battle-cruisers had not been annihilated, mainly thanks to the action of a single man. Scheer and von Hipper had also escaped, to be crowned on their return with glory and honour. The surface

The German battle-cruiser *Seydlitz* burning after Jutland   *photo:* *Imperial War Museum*   IWM

sea warfare had reached, and passed, its climax. The German fleet came out again in August and October 1916, and in a final sortie in April 1918. All appearances were abortive.

Later, the sphere of decision shifted. The protracted duel between German U-boats and Allied merchant shipping became the most critical of the entire war. Thanks, in the end, to the protection of convoy, the merchantmen won, but as Wellington remarked about Waterloo it was 'the nearest run thing you ever saw in your life'. Little more than thirty years later, the undersea pattern was to repeat itself on an equally intense scale.

If there were to be no more Jutlands, there was a tragic aftermath. This was the death of Field-Marshal Lord Kitchener in the cruiser *Hampshire*, which had been present at the battle. The *Hampshire*, carrying Kitchener and his party to Russia, struck a mine off Marwick Head in Orkney at about 7.40 pm on 5 June, only a handful of men surviving the sinking and the prevailing high seas. The mine had been laid by the German U-75 on the night of 28–9 May, with the object of hampering British concentration by endangering the exits from Jellicoe's fleet base at Scapa. Ironically, Lieutenant-Commander Kurt Beitzen had sown the mine in the wrong place, but the result could not have been more sensational. The nation had much to mourn that distant June.

Bibliography

The larger number of the works listed below are by deeply valued friends of the present writer. Some are living; others, alas, are now dead. The living will know the great extent of my debt to them and how fully their work has been appreciated – o.w.

Chapter 1
William the Silent, C. V. Wedgwood (1944), is admirable for the earlier background. *The Defeat of the Spanish Armada*, Garrett Mattingly (1959), makes use of Dutch material. *The Spanish Armada*, Michael Lewis (1960), is comprehensive on the technical side. *Full Fathom Five: Wrecks of the Spanish Armada*, Colin Martin (1973), includes accounts of recent diving in search of Spanish artefacts.

Chapter 2
The Great Dutch Admirals, J. B. de Liefde (trans: 1873), has biographies of Tromp, de Ruyter and others. *Robert Blake: General at Sea*, J. R. Powell (1972), contains the harvest of a lifetime of study. *The Anglo-Dutch Wars of the 17th Century*, C. R. Boxer (1974), though in modest booklet form, has a wealth of illustrations from the National Maritime Museum and a bibliography of the principal English and Dutch printed sources.

Chapter 3
The fullest work in English bearing on the subject of this chapter is *Naval Wars in the Baltic*, R. C. Anderson (1910; reprinted 1969).

Chapter 4
The best modern edition of George Anson's *A Voyage Round the World* is edited by Glyndwr Williams (1974). *Documents Relating to Anson's Voyage Round the World 1740–1744*, ed. for the Navy Records Society by Glyndwr Williams (1967), is full on the official side. *Log of the Centurion*, ed. Leo Heaps (1973), contains the notes kept by Captain Philip Saumarez. Dr Samuel Johnson made a digest of Anson's voyage for the *Gentleman's Magazine* (1749), vol XIX, in which Benjamin Robins is mentioned as having 'the chief hand' in the narrative as published.

Chapter 5
I am greatly indebted to an account by Nicholas Tracy 'The Capture of Manila' which was printed in *The Mariner's Mirror*, vol 55, no 3 (Journal of the Society for Nautical Research: 1969). Dr Tracy's article was based on a longer consideration he prepared in 1967 for the University of Southampton.

The Naval Chronicle (1801), vol V, p 281; (1804), vol XII, p 442; and (1808) vol XX, p 337 contains descriptions of the capture of the *Santissima Trinidada* in 1762, also some account of the career of Admiral Cornish and his nephew.

Chapter 6

Outstandingly the best biography of Rodney is *Rodney*, David Spinney (1968). For the later battle, *St Vincent and Camperdown*, Christopher Lloyd (1963) covers background and personalities. *A Narrative of the Battle of Cape St Vincent*, Colonel Drinkwater Bethune (1797 and 1840; reprinted 1969), is full of picturesque detail.

Chapter 7

Rodney, David Spinney (1968) is invaluable, as is *British Admirals of the Eighteenth Century: Tactics in Battle*, John Creswell (1972), which covers sailing tactics in general.

Chapter 8

An account of Howe's battle appears in *The Glorious First of June*, Oliver Warner (1961). *Logs of the Great Sea Fights*, vol I, ed. T. Sturges Jackson, (Navy Records Society: 1899) is valuable.

Chapter 9

A monumental work on the attack in 1801 is *The Great Gamble: Nelson at Copenhagen*, Dudley Pope (1972). An account of the 1807 attack appears in *A Naval History of England*, vol II, G. J. Marcus (1971). Wellington's part in this affair is described in *Wellington: the Years of the Sword*, Elizabeth Longford (1969). *The Saumarez Papers*, ed. A. N. Ryan (Navy Records Society: 1968) describes in detail the effect of British intervention in the Baltic during the Napoleonic War.

Chapter 10

The most authoritative recent account of Jutland is contained in *From the Dreadnought to Scapa Flow*, vol III (5 vols) Professor Arthur Marder (1961–70). *Beatty*, Rear-Admiral W. S. Chalmers (1951), includes eyewitness scenes on board HMS *Lion* during the progress of the battle of 1916. Also most useful is *The Battle of Jutland*, Geoffrey Bennett (1964). I must acknowledge valued help received for this chapter from the staff of the Royal Marines Museum at Eastney and from Canon W. M. Lummis MC.

Index